Iru

PRAISE FOR *IRU: THE REMARKABLE LIFE OF IRAWATI KARVE*

'This is a fantastic, beautifully written, biography of one of India's most remarkable scholars, Irawati Karve. Founded on deep research but written like a novel, the book is moving and inspiring, and filled with empathy and insight. Through the story of Iru, we learn about the educated Marathi milieu of the first three-quarters of the 20th century, the diffusion of anthropometric racial science from metropoles like Berlin, and the frugality and dedication required by academic research. We also see how the sociologist and essayist Karve understood the lives of Indian women, her love for birds and nature, and her wide-ranging interests. Thiago and Urmilla make such a seamless team, it is hard to see where the research of one begins and the writing of the other ends. I am sure *Iru* will be a classic.'

—Nandini Sundar, Professor, Sociology,
University of Delhi

Iru

The Remarkable Life of Irawati Karve

URMILLA DESHPANDE

THIAGO PINTO BARBOSA

SPEAKING TIGER BOOKS LLP
125A, Ground Floor, Shahpur Jat, near Asiad Village,
New Delhi 110049

First published by Speaking Tiger in 2024

ISBN: 978-93-5447-847-5
eISBN: 978-93-5447-802-4

10 9 8 7 6 5 4 3 2 1

To:

Saheli
Sukhi
Alec
Ralf
Ashish
Chanda
Nandu mama
Nadia
Noorie
Maxine maushi
Rajani maushi
Mithoo
Ruby
Christy
Tim
Surindar
Manju
Meena mami
Samira
Gavan
Sai maushi
Tissa
Frank-Udo
Ben
Stephanie
Jai maushi
Nandini
Priya
Madhura
Zia
Winnie

and all of Iru's family who are here and all who are still to come:

This book is for you.

'Our history shows that in every century, new people have come and made India their home...It is a fascinating subject for study to try to find out what we are—Indians as a whole, but it is entirely wrong to imagine ancestries and base claims on territories as somehow one's own.

All those who are in India today, who feel it is their homeland are Indians...The society we want to build is not a Hindu society or a Hindi society but a multi-cultural, multilingual society which has knowledge of one another's culture and has decided to live and work together in comradeship.'

—Irawati Karve in
'The Racial Factor in Indian Social Life', 1963

Contents

A Note from the Authors

Irawati Karve is one of India's best known anthropologists, besides being the first woman to lecture in social sciences in India. Although she was a pioneer in her field, it can be said that she is only vaguely remembered, in her own country and in her own science. This is one of the reasons that we embarked on this work, but also, more importantly, because we felt that Irawati Karve has valuable, important, even urgent things to say to us today.

Irawati Karve's oeuvre, from her works on kinship to her essays on Indian culture, is vast. She has authored dozens and dozens of papers, published in scientific journals as well as magazines and newspapers, and spoken in many public events and radio interviews. She wrote books widely read by anthropologists working in or on South Asia, like *Kinship Organisation in India*[1] or *Hindu Society*,[2] as well as a book that reached far beyond academic circles—and can still be found in bookstores in India today—*Yuganta*,[3] her collection of critical essays on the Mahabharata.

Irawati lived in a time when science and politics went through devastating changes. Seen from today's perspective, her work is not exempt from ambivalences and even some controversy. Trained in a school of racist science in Berlin at the dawn of Nazism, she challenged her German colleagues and defied theories of white superiority, and later struggled to adapt what she had learnt to study Indians in a non-racist way. She was also criticized by none other than Louis Dumont—famous French scholar of all things Indian—for giving the Mahabharata historical importance.

Academics learn and grow in the public sphere and are judged long after they are gone. We can only interpret the life and work and imagine the future trajectory of a brilliant woman who died all too soon: before she had concluded her work and her intellectual growth. While Karve's words need to be understood in her historical context, we believe that a lot of what she said and wrote, saw and lived, in her short but remarkable life has a lot to teach us about the state of the world.

In order to arrive at this narrative we travelled to Mumbai, Delhi, Pune, Phaltan, Berlin, London and Berkeley. We researched archives in various libraries, universities, and institutions in these cities, and online. We used all the obvious sources we could, and, as happens when you step into the world with a purpose, we came across some unexpected sources as well. For Thiago, Irawati Karve herself was a discovery in an archive of a building that was no longer what it used to be when she was there. For Urmilla, apart from a lifetime of knowledge that comes from being Irawati's granddaughter, an old duffel bag untouched for two decades in her late mother's cupboard turned out to be photographs that were nearly dust, all belonging to Irawati and Dinkar Karve.

We have both talked with Irawati's family members, including her daughter Jai Nimbkar, who is now ninety years old and, she says, tired of talking about her mother. Irawati's son, Anand Karve, well known in his own right, shared his memories of his mother and his life with her. Maxine

Berntsen, whom Irawati considered a daughter, and who worked on the translation of *Yuganta* into English, shared her knowledge and insights. K.C. Malhotra gave generously of his time and memories, as did B.V. Bhanu and R.K. Mutatkar, as well as many Indian anthropologists who never met her but were inspired by her work, including Nandini Sundar and Shantanu Ozarkar. We also found traces of Irawati in many different historical records: in the archive of the Max Planck Society in Berlin (which holds many letters she sent to her German ex-colleagues), in the archive of the Berlin university where she did her PhD, in university libraries in Pune and Berkeley, as well as in the archive of the Rockefeller Foundation, which sponsored Irawati's two-month-long tour across America. Irawati's own essays were an invaluable resource—they are filled with insights and details about her family, her travels, and her philosophy.

All the memories, the stories, long and short, that we collected from people, and letters, photographs, books, and papers, were woven together in our critical fabulation. The result is this book: a historical and personal narrative about the remarkable figure that is Irawati.

Prologue

Berlin, 1929

Human skulls are not smooth. Jagged seams run along the bony plates that form the curves of the human head. The skulls on the table had been examined and measured, as had over a hundred others. It had taken months to come to the conclusion that she had come to. She sat there, by a window, the fading light of a short winter day touching her face and hair, quite unaware of the world outside. She was turned inward, thinking about what she was about to write, and what that might mean for her immediate, and distant future.

The hypothesis must have been abhorrent to her, but it was the one she had had to prove. European skulls, when measured, would show asymmetry, because the right lobe of the European brain was overdeveloped. Logic and reason sat in the right lobe of the brain, and Europeans were logical. This must cause an asymmetry in the skull itself, which she would surely find when she measured European skulls. She also had to measure non-European skulls, which, presumably, would be symmetrical on the sagittal plane, because, not having the superior powers of reasoning of white people, the brains of non-Europeans would not have an overdeveloped right lobe.

She, a young, non-European woman, had measured the skulls of Europeans and non-Europeans for her PhD project, and after months of detailed examination and mensuration she had to now present her conclusion. But how?

She sighed. It would be what it was. Her conclusion went against her supervisor's hypothesis, against the accepted thinking of the institute, and of the scientific community. She had been instructed to prove the hypothesis, not disprove it. What would her professor and colleagues say? Perhaps she would go home without the degree she had come so far for, so far and so alone. From the first time she went to school, through all those years to this one, she had fought for her education, year by year. She could almost not bear the thought that she would return without the title before her name. But, doctor or not, she was a scientist. And this was the truth her work had brought her to: Asymmetries did not belong to any particular group of people, or 'race'. Nor did symmetries. Silently below this conclusion sat the other words that made her smile. She picked the skull nearest her and held it up like Hamlet: 'Logic and reason don't belong to any particular group of people either,' she said out loud.

Irawati Karve's PhD supervisor, Professor Eugen Fischer, would not have had to read Irawati's entire thesis to know what it contained. She had stated her conclusion bluntly, right in her title:

Die normale Asymmetrie des Menschlichen Schädels: The Normal Asymmetry of the Human Skull.

Part One

1

Ausland

The Port of Bombay, June of the year 1927. The heavy cloud cover felt oppressive, as if the sky had settled onto the grimy asphalt of the city. Under the low sky, a symphony made up of so many individual sounds—the hum of ships, the occasional cry of gulls, the shuffling of feet, and the incessant chatter of dockyard labour and hundreds of passengers lined up to board a steamship that would take them to the Port of Hamburg. Among them a young woman with pale translucent skin, and grey-green eyes framed by round, silver-rimmed glasses stood taller than most of the people around her. Her hair, parted in the centre, formed a severely straight line down the top of her head, tied into a knot at the nape of her neck. She wore a pastel saree, the pallu held in place with a silver bar pinned at the shoulder to a white shirt, crisp that morning, but wilted now in the humidity and her own perspiration. She was almost as tall as her husband, the tall, dark, handsome man beside her, his black wavy hair combed straight back from a broad forehead, his square-jawed open face prone to a quick smile. They had travelled together to Bombay by train from their hometown, Pune. They did not hold hands, but looked directly into each other's eyes as they talked. They had been married less than a year.

Irawati Karve waited with her husband, Dinkar, who had once made this journey himself, to board the passenger steamship that would take her to Germany to study for her PhD. If she was nervous, she did not show it. There was a determination about them both, the same determination that had brought them here, against the wishes of her own father, and against the wishes, explicitly expressed, by Irawati's father-in-law, Dinkar's father, the venerable and immensely respected patriarch, champion of women's rights and education, Maharshi Dhondo Keshav Karve. This was a peculiar turn of events that was both unpleasant and unexpected. Even so, here they were: Irawati, at the beginning of another adventure in her remarkable life, and Dinu, to see her off, to cheer her on, to support her, to encourage her, to be her champion, now as he would be through the rest of their life together. He was letting her go, not in the sense of giving her permission—he was letting her go because he adored and admired her. She looked into his concerned, kind face one last time, as he said to her, 'Don't forget to cover your ears, Iru my dear, it will get very cold when the winter comes.' She only nodded as she turned away from him to walk up the long ramp with all the other passengers, and she was surprised by the sting in her eyes. Whether that was because she was leaving her husband, her many brothers, her dearest friend, and her entire homeland behind, or because everything coalesced into her throat and eyes at that moment as she began on this journey into the world, she did not know. It was the first time of many that she would leave this shore in her lifetime, the very first time, at the age of twenty-two. Above all though, she looked forward. This, after all, was the culmination of all the pleading and threatening and cajoling she had had to perform, her fight for every year of education since the sixth year at school. When she returned, that quest would be complete.

The steamship did not originate there. It had arrived at the port of Bombay on its way from Australia to Europe, having stopped in Colombo in what was then Ceylon. When Irawati boarded her ship, it was full of passengers speaking a cacophony of languages. Although two or three weeks is a long time to be confined on a vessel with people not of one's choosing, she would have enjoyed listening and talking to her fellow passengers. Irawati was a lifelong listener. She engaged with everyone she met, on trains and buses, in shops, while waiting to cross the street, in lines at the bank or the library. And people chatted with her. She had authority softened by an easy smile and non-judgemental curiosity, and there were few who did not answer her many questions, sometimes very personal ones. She spoke some German by the time she left, her work and studies in the science of anthropology in Berlin would be done in that language. Dinu's German was flawless, and after she returned home and started a family, it would eventually become their language: the one they spoke when they had private conversations in public, or when a grandchild was present. But on that steamship would be the first time she would be able to practise with native German speakers.

The monsoon had begun, the ship was restless all through the first part of the voyage: stormy winds roiled the Arabian Sea, and rain poured down the windows. On the open sea, the view was a restless palette of wet, angry greys. At that early stage of the voyage, it could have been a period of trepidation and anxiety for Irawati. She was alone, she had left her husband, and her family and friends, and the shores of home, for what would be a long time. Irawati's energy and thoughts, however, were focused on her severely seasick cabinmate. The turbulent wind and rain caused the vessel to pitch and roll ceaselessly, and had affected the lady terribly. The food did not help matters. For Irawati, a Chitpavan Brahmin woman who had never eaten the flesh of any animal, bird, or fish, there was not much to eat but potatoes, and vegetables that were so severely cooked that they were barely recognizable as plants. The meal she enjoyed the most was breakfast, with fresh breads baked in the galley, fruity spreads, and salty butter. She became thoroughly addicted too to the coffee whose aroma greeted her as she entered the dining saloon. Every morning she thought about eating the eggs, but put it off for the next day, and the next. There were strips of pink meat, and at dinnertime sometimes she saw thick brown sausages on the plates of other people at the table, and she was surprised that the smell did not offend her, in fact, she found it quite pleasant.

Irawati took buttered slices of bread from breakfast, and mashed potatoes from dinner for her cabinmate, but the poor lady was incapable of keeping any food down. She retched violently and often, because there was nothing left for her to bring up, and, giving her sips of water that she heaved up within minutes of swallowing them, Irawati asked her again and again what she could do to help. All the poor woman could say was, 'Make it stop, just for a moment, make it stop.'

Irawati herself may have got her ocean legs in Burma, when she was a little girl, travelling on the waterways there with her parents and brothers. She would recall this poor woman's plight when she herself was an unhappy passenger in a car crossing the Bay Bridge in San Francisco. But that would be three decades into the future. Thankfully, on her way to Germany, she was not seasick, the motion of the ship did not affect her at all. It was a promising start to a voyage that would take weeks, and a journey that would form her academic mind.

Ships enter the Elbe from its mouth, and follow it into the belly of Hamburg, to the great river port. For a passenger coming here, even if they had sailed into a port before, this was a unique place. Hamburg could be heard long before it was seen. The hum of vessels, the low grinding of the metal gear-teeth of loading machines, thumping and booming, clicking and whining, metal against metal, people and commerce, and, filling in any gaps in that wall of sound was thc soft wind harassing the water, and the seabirds wheeling overhead, filling the sky.

This part of the journey was almost over. From Hamburg, she would take two trains to get to Berlin. Standing on the deck, Irawati took in everything. She had seen a harbour like this before, she had felt the feeling before, of connection to the world, as if the heart of the world was beating somewhere, and she was afloat on one artery among thousands on its body. Hamburg of 1927 did not smell or even look like the Rangoon of her childhood, but the feeling was the same. Coming and going beside the steamer were vessels of every shape and size and purpose, from sailboats to huge goods carriers. People on the decks of passenger steamers waved at her and she waved back, along with her fellow passengers, every one of them was part of the same excitement, the same sense of wonder, as they sailed into the port of Hamburg.

Irawati walked down the huge ramp, and onto the quayside. After weeks on the water, she took her first step onto the ground, and stood still. She felt the certainty of the unmoving ground, and yet, she felt uncertain, in an unfamiliar place. Irawati looked up at the seagulls, in their own domain above it all. She had never seen such gulls before, some small and all white, some grey-winged, some huge and brown-speckled, some mid-sized and black-backed, speaking languages she didn't know. Her feeling of being in an alien place was complete. She was far from the monsoon kokil, from the evening crows, the chirruping flocks of sparrows. But, soon enough, she would know these strangers too, and learn their calls.

2

Berlin, Berlin

Irawati had never before seen a metropolis like Berlin. The wide main streets streamed with every conceivable kind of traffic—people on foot and on bicycles, motorcycles with sidecars, cars, horse carts, she once even saw a dog dragging a small wheelbarrow. The vastly varied architecture felt familiar to her at first glance, but not if she looked closer. Fascinating and deep contrasts ran through every aspect of the city. There were opulent buildings, like the new shopping palace that took up a whole city block and had its own metro rail stop, or the enormous restaurants with tables spilling out onto tree-lined sidewalks, and then there were the concrete slums, each with a single street door that led to an endless labyrinth of courtyards, where families were packed into small, unhygienic rooms with several households sharing a single toilet. The incessant sound of human life—couples fighting, babies crying, tired mothers screaming—emanated from within. Irawati noticed the washing hanging out of the windows, the visibly underfed, rickets-ridden children playing in dirty alleyways and yards where the sun never reached them. She was assailed by the smell of boiled cabbage that hung over these tenements, punctuated by the occasional whiff of wurst, and she wondered how they managed. Some four million people crammed into a single city. It was not so different from the city of Bombay, and yet, it was. This city had a dark side to it, a despair that seemed to her to come from another history.

This country Irawati had packed her bags for was perhaps not what she had imagined, or even hoped for. It was, after all, recently vanquished, in a war of its own making. The First World War of 1914-18 that had involved enough states and killed enough people to be called the Great War, had been over for a decade. Although the fighting was done, the aftermath was still felt painfully by the country that had started it. The Treaty of Versailles (signed in 1919, and ratified in 1921), in laying down the terms of reparations, had delivered the revenge of the victorious countries Germany had drawn into what was until then the bloodiest conflict in human history. Germany, assumed to be the instigator and perpetrator of the war, was to disarm, give up territories, and pay reparations that it believed would cripple it financially for decades. In a letter protesting the terms of the treaty, the German government said, 'We were aghast when we read in documents the demands made upon us, the victorious violence of our enemies.'

Not everyone, at the time as well as in the years that followed, has analysed the effects of the treaty in the same way. John Maynard Keynes, one of the earliest critics of the treaty, wrote in 1919 that the closeness of the countries involved, both geographically and economically, meant that making Germany pay enormous reparations would negatively affect all of them. In Germany, it was referred to as the *Diktat* of Versailles, a fitting term considering that Germany itself had almost no say in the terms of the treaty. After an initial period of economic and political instability, however, the country could have been called stable, if not prosperous. It would not stay that way through Irawati's time there. Life in Germany, as Irawati came to know, and Berlin itself, was hard for much of the population. Poverty, crime, a growing political climate of unease and instability, all contributed to an exciting, if restless atmosphere.

By the time Irawati became a temporary citizen of Berlin, it was a thrilling, and perhaps difficult city. Fritz Lang's *Metropolis*, which would reach into the next century of science fiction cinema, was released in that year. The Bauhaus school was leaking design ideas into the commercial mainstream, Alfred Döblin was writing *Berlin Alexanderplatz*, his great novel about the city, and Josephine Baker was dancing joyfully wearing nothing but pearls and a skirt made of bananas. Although Irawati was familiar with the work of her brother-in-law, R.D. Karve, in the area of public sexual and reproductive health and his views on women's right to sexual freedom and pleasure, his was a one-man enterprise, and one that was thoroughly frowned upon. In her new city, Magnus Hirschfield's *Institut für Sexualwissenschaft* was doing invaluable work on sexual health and reproduction, and also on what he then termed sexual transitions (homosexuality) and transvestism and transsexuality (terms that Hirschfield himself invented). Hirschfield was of the quite progressive view for that time that homosexuality was inborn and natural, rather than a morally repugnant illness. Together with his medical colleagues, they even offered sex reassignment surgery. The institute would, tragically, be violently attacked in 1933, and all their research and documents burned by Hitlerjugend—Hitler Youth—the youth organisation of the Nazi Party. The Nazis tried to snuff out everything that Berlin, and the world could have been: the art, the music, the literature, and the artists, the musicians, the writers and philosophers themselves as well. But, as yet, while Irawati was a Berlin citizen in the anxious but liberal, Utopianistic 1920s, the Nazi party had little influence or following.

At the time she was there, it seemed as if Germany was suddenly free of its past, free to express itself in ways that were so ground-breaking and unique that the reverberations and influences, positive, and also negative, are still with us today, and will always be. In cinema, art, architecture, science, and literature—in every aspect of culture and human endeavour, the rich moment of Weimar Republic Germany cast its shadow, its spell. This was the decade that would be called the golden twenties. In some ways, it was also a hopeful time: Germany got a seat at the League of Nations, the terms of reparations were being reconsidered, peace in Europe seemed likely. The poverty and misery seemed at times temporary. But during Irawati's time there, Hitler's star did begin its rise. Irawati would write, years later,[4] that Germany seemed to her a country seething with anger over the dismissal of their 'just and reasonable' demands to the League of Nations, and their unfair treatment by Britain and France in the drafting of the Versailles treaty. She, like many Germans, saw the post war period as a lost opportunity—a moment to bring Germany into the world that was squandered because of selfishness and then fear, which Germany laid at the feet of other European nations, America, and even the whole world. And all that marvellous, forward-thinking art and social freedoms did not stop the great tragedy that was unfolding and tearing at the fabric of the Weimar Republic.

If there was anything about Berlin that disturbed Irawati, it was the beggars. The city was full of them. They were not the kind of beggars that beleaguered her in India, where she was particularly irked by those that gathered outside temples and around religious sites. She encountered these when she went on her pilgrimages to Pandharpur, Jejuri, Badri Kedar—all over India. In her writings, she says that for her the beauty of the Himalayan landscapes was marred by this practice of ordinary people, children of local farmers and shopkeepers, constantly following pilgrims and begging. Charity gets you credit in heaven, so people gave alms, and so people begged. This was not the case in 1927 Berlin, where the beggars were war-torn men. Irawati had seen lepers, and cripples too, but in Berlin she saw the most horrific injuries that a person could experience and still live. These were men from the Great War, a war in which it was common for limbs to be lost to gangrene in the trenches and faces blown off in artillery fire or mines. Not just mines that soldiers stepped on, but ones that were tunnelled below the trenches, ones that killed, some say, the lucky ones. Those that lived had wounds that left men—and they were almost all men—unable to work, unable to support themselves by any means other than begging. Some of these men got to their daily begging spots by themselves, some were brought there every day by transport. In Berlin, like elsewhere in the world where the war had created such men, begging was a livelihood. She saw them in every part of the city as she went about her life in Berlin. But she did not have enough spare coins for them.

~

Summer in Berlin was delightful. Irawati took long walks in the many parks that were actually small forests within the city. Parts of it reminded her of Pune, but only superficially.

The trees were not the same, nor the birds. There was no way that she, who knew gulmohar from peepal and banyan, and kokil from crow, could pretend she was in Pune. Nor did she want to. She learned the German names of the trees and birds of Berlin, she collected leaves from the linden and the chestnut, and looked for bird feathers on her walks. She began to know them, woodpeckers—specht, the tiny red-breasted robin—rotkehlchen, the corvids—crow and elster—the big, flashy magpie. She was startled by these huge black and white corvids at first, and found that they were not well liked. She could see why, they were jaunty and spoke German—a loud harsh and insistent chatter heard all day, everywhere.

Early one Sunday morning, she was out walking on a mostly deserted road when she saw a small child looking up at the sky. She looked too, and saw them. Row upon row of Eurasian cranes, moving like dark lace against the sky, making sweet crooning sounds as they flew south. After that she knew to look up when she heard their unmistakable sound, talking to each other as they travelled south, and then north again after the winter, over the city.

The sky over Berlin surprised Irawati with more than cranes. Fighter pilots, left with nothing to do after the Versailles treaty decreed that 'armed forces of Germany must not include any military or naval air forces', did air shows at Tempelhofer Feld, Berlin's airport. And on August 16, 1929, the Graf Zeppelin, a strange and unlikely aircraft, hovered over the Brandenburg gate like an enormous airborne vegetable, a sight not many that saw it ever forgot.

Every city she had lived in had a river flowing through it. The Spree was not a big mighty river in Berlin, but the riverfront feeling once felt, stayed within her forever. Irawati would stand on a bridge and watch couples picnicking in longboats alongside families of mallards as they passed beneath her. There were swans on the Spree and its canals. She had seen swans only in photographs, and to see them floating imperiously on the river, and on the lakes too, was thrilling. Berlin is also a city of lakes. Weissensee, Wansee, and, if she took the train east as far as it went without leaving the city limits, Müggelsee, where people went to picnic, and sunbathe and swim.

One Friday afternoon, when the anatomy class was unexpectedly cancelled, she and some fellow students went together to visit the Wertheim department store. It was an enormous palace of consumerism, though it was by no means the largest store in the city. The Karstadt store was so big it had a dedicated U-Bahn station.

'These places are all owned by the Jews, you know,' one of the German students in the group said. He pointed out some of the foods and items in the store that were meant only for 'Juden'.

'We should buy from Germans,' they would say, as if German Jews were not German. It wasn't the first time she had encountered this kind of sentiment, it was quite normal for people to speak this way. It disturbed her, but she neither knew how to address it, nor wanted to. It wasn't her country, it wasn't her fight, after all. Even the usurped and mutilated swastika, which had startled her when she first saw it, was theirs now. She put it out of her mind and wandered away from the others. With the help of a shop lady, she bought herself a bathing suit. She was that rare Indian woman who had learned to swim, along with her brothers. She was a good swimmer, with a strong unhurried breaststroke of the time—head always above the water, so that the hair stayed dry, and water didn't get in the eyes. It was the pre-goggles era of swimming, at least for recreational swimmers. She had not, until then, accepted invitations from friends and colleagues, but she would, now that she had a suit. She would swim with the swans in Berlin.

The autumn took Irawati's breath away. Back home, she had seen garnet-coloured leaves on trees in the springtime—she thought of that as the colour of new leaves. As the days grew noticeably shorter, and the trees gave up their green to shades of fire and gold, she enjoyed this season in spite of the deepening cold.

Oma invited her to a special dinner one cool fall weekend, and she was glad to go. This old German lady was like a tiny, fragile, china figurine, with her pale, pale skin, light blue eyes, wispy hair, her pearls and her soft ways. Oma—German for grandmother—was what Irawati had called her from the moment they met, because that's what Dinu called her. She had taught Dinu his flawless German, and she adored him. So she had taken Irawati under her wing immediately. She arranged for Irawati to stay with a Berlin family on her arrival, and later, her rental apartment at Kaiserdamm, in the central Berlin-Charlottenburg. She was well connected, so she recommended Irawati to professors and universities, and she was also well read and knowledgeable. She knew a lot about India and Hindu philosophy. Irawati visited her every other Saturday, and all the holidays, and always enjoyed it. Irawati thought of Oma as a proper Berlin lady. An archetypal German lady, the best of them.

Irawati was not the only guest at dinner that night. She was introduced, and kissed on the cheek by the ladies, and had her hand kissed or shaken by the men. She thought how much she preferred the self-contained and polite namaskar, involving no bodily contact. She thought about how many people she had been introduced to at her own wedding, not so long ago. She was glad she didn't have to kiss or be kissed by all those people. She had made namastes to the younger people, and touched the feet of her elders.

The dining room was warm and glinted with all the polished flatware and gold-rimmed plates, and they all sat down. The chatter quietened when Oma came out of the kitchen with a big silver domed platter and set it down on her end of the table. She uncovered it, and everyone sighed appreciatively. Irawati gasped, and, much to her own horror, began to weep silently. Oma came around behind her.

'My dear,' she said, rubbing Irawati's back and head, 'There isn't anything else to eat in the winter. You'll have to, you know, you can't survive on sauerkraut and gürkchen.' Till then, Irawati had stuck to eating the few vegetable dishes that were available: Potatoes—roasted, boiled, mashed, a dish of potatoes sautéed with onion called Bratkartoffeln. Cabbage—green in butter, red shredded with hints of caraway seed, and yes, sauerkraut, and yes, the pickled cucumbers, the gürkchen. And of course, the beautiful dense breads, with butter or cheese or preserved fruit spreads. It was not so bad as all that. Dinu had eaten and drunk everything from the first day he was in Germany. Vegetables, meats, beer, mulled wine, pickled fish, everything. He had tried to prepare her for it too, she had known that she would have to eat the meat.

'She's a Hindu, a Brahmin,' Oma explained to the other guests, who—educated women and men that they were—nodded understandingly.

The anthropology program that Irawati had been accepted into was taught at the medical faculty, and required that she take zoology, and anatomy. She had had her anatomy class only the day before, and she had stood next to a human corpse, and had to take part in the dissection of it. And now, this.

The huge shoulder of roast beef sat in its juices surrounded by potatoes and carrots, and Oma began to slice and serve it. She carved a very thin slice for Irawati, and smothered it with extra brown gravy from the silver boat. Irawati cut a piece and put it in her mouth. She had never eaten the flesh of any animal, let alone a cow, until then. She chewed it slowly, and swallowed it, and then finished all the food on her plate. She didn't think about it again. She was no longer a vegetarian, after that, not in Germany, nor anywhere else. Oma taught her how to cook many German meat and fish dishes and by the time she went back home, she knew how to roast a shoulder herself, and make the gravy too. Cooking was a skill she carried back with her, and it stood her in good stead, in years to come.

~

Kaiserdamm is a long, wide, divided federal road on the Western side of Berlin. Irawati did not ascertain this as fact, but she was convinced it was the longest and widest thoroughfare in the city. Irawati's apartment was on the corner of a cross street on Kaiserdamm, a few steps from the U-Bahn station. Oma's acquaintance Dr Wenkelbach rented places to students, and she had put in a word for Irawati. The apartment had one room, a small kitchen, and a bathroom. She was on an upper floor, and had a large window from which she could look down into a courtyard formed by the three wings of the building at Kaiserdamm 88. It was close to shops and city parks, and though her building was older, there were newer buildings in the Bauhaus style on

Kaiserdamm. They seemed smooth and clean compared to the wedding-cake moulding and Gothic style architecture of colonial buildings in Bombay and Pune.

The area where she lived was busy, noisy as a city should be. People in cars, vendors with animal-powered carts, students on bicycles, crowds in buses, young men riding loud motorcycles, like Bombay and Pune, but of course not quite. The voices of the people, their sounds and intonation, were quite different. Marathi has its own harsh and throaty sounds, but German was another matter. Even the crows of Berlin, though at first glance could be mistaken for the ones back home, were not the same at all. The black on the Indian crow was neat and tidy, a clean edge where it met the grey part of the plumage. The Berlin crows looked as if they had dipped their heads in black ink, they were more ragged, and their call too, was different.

Some days, when she had time between classes and research and social visits, Irawati took the long walk from home to Uhlandstraße 179. She listened to the conversations of people as she walked. Her German was, by then, almost as good as Dinu's. She was taking classes in zoology, anatomy, anthropology, and doing all her work, and her dissertation, in German. Even the Sanskrit course she was taking was taught by a German professor—it was a German University after all.

At Uhlandstraße, close to the corner of the always bustling Kurfürstensdam (which they called Ku'damm), she walked into the building and down the corridor to a large room. She could see through the glass-paned doors that the room was full of people sitting at the tables draped in white cloths. When she opened the door she smiled, because she was suddenly in a different world, far away from Berlin. The lilts and undulations of Hindi, Bengali, Tamil, and of course

English, and the gorgeous smell of milk tea and familiar spices filled the room. This was the tearoom of Hindustan House, a meeting place for South Asian students. A few of them were her classmates.[5] She sat where she found a spot, and joined in the discussions at the table. Some had news from home, some talk was political and distinctly activist. This could never happen at a university in England, where the authorities had started to keep an eye on activities of students from the colonies. She herself could have gone to England for her studies, it would have been so much easier, and not just because she would not have had to learn a difficult language. As a subject of the British Empire, she would have found it easier to get there and live there. But she, and Dinu, like all the subjects of the empire gathered at that tearoom in Berlin, had made that anti-colonial choice. Some of these students, including her, were in Germany on scholarships and other incentives given by the Weimar government, whose policy it was to lure students from the British and French colonies as a means of undermining the authority of those governments.[6]

She didn't always join in the conversations, she listened to the discussions that took place around her. These young men, and they were mostly men, would have been arrested and jailed if they had been talking insurgency in their homelands. They were imagining the end of the British Empire, freedom for their people, and even how they could best help bring it about, from without and within. Irawati could see that the German policy—of giving colonised youth the ability to think about their colonisation openly—was working. There they were: dreaming about independence, conspiring and fomenting rebellion over tea and samosas in Hindustan House, and at universities all over Germany.

3

Skulls and Bones

The Kaiserdamm U-Bahn station was around the corner from the apartment building. Irawati joined hundreds of women and men in their hurried walk to work each weekday morning. People dressed very well for work, the women in smart dresses and beautiful hats, the men in solemn-coloured suits, and long coats as the weather began to change.

'Guten Morgen.'

Irawati didn't expect a reply, and she didn't receive one. The man was there every morning when she came out, propped against the sun-warmed stone blocks of the building wall, on the right side of the door, and she had to pass him when she turned right to walk to Kaiserdamm station, so she couldn't not wish him, and she couldn't bring herself to pretend to ignore him, so that became the ritual every morning, her greeting, his silence. He was always gone when she came home in the evening, so she wondered about him, where he lived, why he chose to beg at that particular spot in the whole sprawling city each day but Sunday, whether the coins thrown in his can were enough for his Abendbrot—his 'evening bread', the evening meal. Why she hadn't felt that way about the people in Rangoon, or Bombay, or Pune, at railway stations and bus stops, those outside temples profiting from devotees buying cheap karma points, as deformed, as poor, as ugly as this man—she couldn't say. She also couldn't say why she had reacted the way she had the first time she laid eyes on this man. Her mouth had gone dry, and she had to clench her teeth to stop herself from letting the sound of her own horror escape from her. She had quickly averted her eyes and hurried away, to get away, and to catch her train.

She had seen many mangled humans. So many were branded into memory by the heat of shock, faces and bodies she would rather forget. Why else would Burmese villagers misshapen from childhood malnutrition or starved in droughts, grown adults with tiny microcephaly heads in Pune, men with blunted noses and missing fingertips in Bombay, their feet tied in rags exuding that nauseating rot-sweet stench of leprosy, why would all this stay with her for any reason other than that she could not forget? All these people, though, had not prepared her for the man she now wished a good morning every weekday.

As the months passed, she had become accustomed to that face she had once almost fainted at the sight of. The huge pink hole that was his nose and mouth, the entirety of his lower jawbone and teeth exposed on his left side, a part of his eye visible to her, looking at her from under skin melted like wax, she was used to it now. She saw him as a person now, a man who had returned home from a nearby European battlefield, seared by unimaginable heat from the outside and from within. The second day she came out of the building, she looked him straight in his mismatched eyes, and wished him a good morning. She did it every day after that. He never replied.

~

Irawati's final train stop, in a southwestern suburb of Berlin called Dahlem, was Thielplatz station, with its modest but charming arched brick herringbone front entrance, adorned with a giant golden clock. From there it was a short walk through quiet, tree-lined residential streets to Ihnestrasse 22.

The Kaiser Wilhelm Institute for Anthropology, Human Heredity and Eugenics (KWI-A) was a pleasant building inside and out. White outer walls with many large windows, a half circle of stone steps at the main entrance door that led into a bright interior of a long passageway with offices and classrooms, with doors of warm wood, and a stairway leading to the upper floors with more classrooms, offices, and labs. Here Irawati took some classes, and did much of her PhD research, under the supervision of Professor Eugen Fischer.

Eugen Fischer was a German scientist who wrote the textbook on eugenics when this ideological and scientific movement (also called *Rassenhygiene* or race hygiene in Germany) was not yet associated with Hitler's ideas of Aryan racial purity. From 1928, Fischer headed the Berlin and Germany Race Hygiene Societies. Although he originally felt that the National Socialists were 'using false theories of Aryan racial purity for anti-Semitic and nationalist ends,' not only did he compromise, he did something that, in 1933, would make him the first party-appointed university rector: he joined the Nazi Party. The party that, based on those same false theories, would murder some twenty million souls. Adolf Hitler, while doing jail time after his failed coup against the Weimar government in 1923, read Eugen Fischer's work, and used it in his *Mein Kampf*.

This man, whose ideas and work inspired Hitler's belief in 'racial hygiene' and 'Aryan superiority', was, as they would say in German, Irawati's *Doktorvater*—her doctoral father in

Berlin, for the very thing she was in Germany to do: to earn a PhD in anthropology.

According to a prevailing theory of that time and place, logic and reason resided in the right frontal lobe of the brain. If this was the case, then the right frontal side of the skull would be overdeveloped compared to the other side, in order to accommodate the larger right lobe of the brain, making the skull itself asymmetrical. Eugen Fischer's doctoral assignment for Irawati was not surprising, considering his convictions about 'race' and the superiority of white Europeans. He gave her the task of comparing white European skulls with those of 'other races.' Since white Europeans possessed logic and reason that 'other races' did not possess, so argued the theory, this difference would be visible in the skull measurements. The skulls of non-white, non-Europeans, would presumably not show skull asymmetry. The task that Irawati received from her *Doktorvater* Fischer as her PhD topic was, in other words, to show that white Europeans were logical and reasonable—and hence, superior—and 'other races', which included herself, were not.

So Irawati, in the city of change, the city of divisions, the city of Berlin, at the KWI-A, would examine the skulls of white Europeans, and of non-Europeans whose skulls were here, far away from their origins, stolen from their lands and their people. This distance Irawati had in common with them, but, unlike them, she was here of her own choosing.

~

The train and a walk under old chestnut trees took her to Ihnestrasse 22. She hurried to exchange the warmth inside her coat for a lab coat, thin from overwashing and bleach. She stepped out into the corridor. High ceiling, no windows, it was a long concrete cavern between the archive room and the lab. The sound of her steps multiplied itself off the walls and the ceiling. If she closed her eyes there was a legion of Irawatis in bleached white coats walking with her, each holding a tray with human skulls covered in a bleached white cloth. The tray was heavy, green painted iron. Her wrists trembled, and it was always a relief to put it down on her table.

She lifted the cloth off, folded it, and placed it to the side. She sat down. Then, as she always did, she examined the skulls one by one. All these skulls were from German East Africa—Ruanda, Tanzania, and from Melanesia. She knew what people from these places looked like. She looked into their eye sockets, trying to fill in the eyes, the eyelashes, the skin, the hair, and then, the smile. The person. Sometimes she conjured up a man, sometimes a woman, sometimes a girl, and once, when it was a very small skull, she imagined a baby, who had never walked on its own feet.

The skulls weren't all the same, of course, they were all different, the colours, the shapes, the grooves, the dips. But she knew that neither she, nor anyone else, could tell just by looking at one, whether it had belonged to a dead German soldier, or a murdered Nama woman. She didn't think about that too much, or she wouldn't be able to do this work. But it was always there with her, the sense of violation. An irrational sense that these bones longed to be home.

'Forgive me,' she said softly, as she always did, to each one of those skulls.

The crates of human remains that arrived at the institute went to the basement of the building at Ihnestrasse 22 before being archived in the attic. A large room, bright with windows and overhead globe lamps was the first stop for the bones.

Here they were unpacked and placed in rows on shelves specially made to hold rows of skulls. Students such as Irawati had access to them. The KWI-A archive room held 5,000 individual human remains. Irawati used 149 skulls for her research. Forty-nine of these were from the KWI-A collection, representing different 'racial' backgrounds, including some European skulls. The other 100 skulls she used were housed in the anatomical collection of the Wilhelm University Berlin and like most skulls in the KWI-A were also obtained in a colonial context. Specifically, these 100 skulls came from German colonial expeditions, collected by two anthropologists commissioned by the Berlin Ethnological Museum. Half of these skulls were obtained in Papua New Guinea and Solomon Islands (when these territories were under German colonial rule) and the other half in Rwanda (Germany colonised Tanzania, where the same expedition started). These 100 skulls became part of the anatomical collection of the Wilhelm University in Berlin.

In order to produce skull measurements, Irawati used an instrument called a craniophor. This is essentially a glass box. The skull is set inside it, at a right angle. A transparent paper is placed on the top, on the glass. The skull seen through the paper is then drawn onto the paper. Then a new sheet of paper is placed, and the angle of the skull is changed, drawn again, and so on. Then the differences between all the points on all those pieces of paper are calculated. The work took effort, concentration, and time. It is only one of the myriad human inventions that seem somehow important and scientific, that seem to be generating data that is important and scientific, that will confirm or unravel important theories by scientific method. If the method sounds arcane and reminiscent of palm reading or phrenology—things that many people would be sceptical about today—it is because these do all belong in the same rubbish bin of ideas that humanity is better off discrediting and discarding. But they are still with us, still doing exactly what they were doing then: finding differences between humans, but, more dangerously, assigning meaning and hierarchies to those differences based on the politics of the assigner. Meaning, in this case, Eugen Fischer.

As she held these remains in her hands, what questions would Irawati—a woman, a Hindu, a Brahmin, a colonial subject—ask of what lay before her: about Germany and its colonial project, about Indians, about gender, about religion, about 'race,' about the dead, about herself? And, having asked, how then would she answer them?

~

The genocide and crimes against humanity committed by Nazi Germany are very much part of our consciousness. We think of these words as having always been part of the language of the world. In fact, these terms were invented to describe Germany's acts, by two Jewish lawyers from Kyiv, then part of Poland, whose family and friends and acquaintances and colleagues were murdered by Nazis. It was because of Hersch Lauterpacht and Rafael Lemkin that the terms were used, for the first time in history, at the Nuremberg trials.[7] But though the terms 'genocide' and 'crimes against humanity' did not exist until then, the acts of course always did, all through human history, and German history too.

Depending on how you looked at it, Germany was not the most 'successful' of colonisers. Coming to it after Britain, France, Belgium, Portugal and Spain, among others, and, after the Americas and most of South Asia and Africa had been taken, Germany nevertheless had a quite vast colonial empire. And German colonial subjects, among them the Herero and Nama people in German Southwest Africa, today the country of Namibia, were in a gruesome rehearsal of that other genocide that was yet to come. It was learning, and refining its shape, there in the colonies. Learning from the actions of military men like General Lothar Von Trotta who, after quelling the Boxer rebellion in China, was sent to Africa, where he gave the order for the extermination of the entire Herero and Nama population. It was also learning from scientists like Eugen Fischer, who undertook examinations on the bodies of Africans, particularly children of the so-called (and by some, loathed) 'mixed marriages', born from the unions of white male Dutch settlers and Khoekhoe women in the town of Rehoboth and known as the Rehoboth Basters.[8] 'Racial purity' was already very much part of their thinking, and, more importantly, so too was the intention of these men who feared 'racial degeneration' or what Fischer also called 'bastardization'. This was going where it went: the history we now look back on with horror was unfolding, with the solid foundation of their scientific racism, a racism that emerged with and was justified by, a science based on erroneous assumptions. In German South West Africa, Herero and Nama people were loaded into cattle cars and sent to their deaths, by means of poisoned wells, thirst, starvation, and direct slaughter. Many were also sent to 'concentration camps', a term coined by the Germans for this occasion, like the Shark Island concentration camp, where thousands perished and died. If this reverberates in memory, it is because, long before the 'Final Solution' was conceived in a tranquil villa on the shores of Wansee by Hitler and his minions, it had already been enacted in a German Protectorate in Africa.

The Nama and Herero were nearly exterminated, after courageously rebelling against German colonialism and being repressed, tortured, experimented on, and intentionally starved to death. But even after their death, they were not given the peace or dignity of burials in their homeland. They were reduced to objects for the use of their murderers. The transport of the remains of people became even more urgent after the Treaty of Versailles, which decreed that Germany must give up all its colonies. When it became apparent that this 'scientific resource' would soon be lost, Eugen Fischer himself sent word out to anyone still in the field. Those coming back home, not only scientists, but administrators, soldiers, even ordinary people, took huge quantities of the bones of the dead to bring home with them. Remains from territories under German colonialism including German South West Africa, German East Africa, and German New Guinea in the Pacific, were sent, by the thousands, to Germany. To add insult to injury—or in this case contempt to murder—this gruesome harvest would arrive in crates, be unpacked and shelved, catalogued and numbered, become objects to be displayed in glass-fronted cupboards, subjects of study in scientific institutions and museums, and trophies in private collections, all over Germany. It would be used to further demean the people and the nations it belonged to, to 'prove' the superiority of their white colonisers, based on methods and theories that no longer have any standing in scientific circles.

It was in one such institution that Irawati would find them.

~

The KWI-A where Irawati studied was only one of several institutes of the Kaiser Wilhelm Society. Physics, chemistry and biology institutes among many others in Berlin meant that some of the most prominent scientists of the time lived and worked in Berlin at the same time as Irawati was there, including Max Planck, Niels Bohr, Albert Einstein, and, a woman who Irawati met and came to know, the Austrian physicist, Lise Meitner. As a fellow woman scientist, Lise Meitner might have found Irawati interesting. But she might also have seen this young Indian student as a woman of colour in a space that belonged to a very particular kind of male, of a particular 'race', in need of some support. She would not have been wrong.

Irawati was not initially intimidated by the fact that she was one of the few women, and certainly the only woman of colour, in her classes. She was the only girl among six children growing up, and she thought she knew how to handle herself in that situation. She was a Chitpavan Brahmin in the city of Pune and, whether this troubled her or not, was accustomed to the status and treatment that being at the top of the caste hierarchy brought with it. She had enough confidence, then, to speak her mind. Besides, she was in Germany for higher education, so she assumed that discussion, and even disagreement, or at least questioning, would be welcome, and encouraged. She would find out otherwise. Again and again, she was brushed aside by white male professors when she joined discussions or raised opinions that went against their views, particularly if she attempted to compare the institutions or practices of so-called 'primitive cultures' to their own, as they would have called it, 'civilized culture'.[9] She learned, the hard way, to keep her mouth shut. And although she often felt silenced, she would find ways to express her disagreement—sometimes through the written word.

It was not surprising that someone like Lise Meitner would befriend her, or spend time with her and listen to her experiences as a foreign woman scientist, in many ways like herself, a Jewish woman scientist in a male-dominated and increasingly anti-Semitic zone. Though Irawati never met Lise again after she left Germany, she never really left her behind. And she looked at the world through the gift Lise had given her in Berlin: a Leica camera that she would use to take photographs from Berlin and London, and Himalayan landscapes decades in the future.

4

Darkness Falls

The day was supposed to be as long as the night, it had always been that way, all of her life. And now, when she stepped outside the KWI-A building, or the Wilhelm University where she also took classes, it was dark. At four in the afternoon, when it would be time for a cup of tea or a walk or a swim at the Pune Gym, it was night-time in Berlin. It was dark. And before darkness fell the day had been mostly grey. She walked to the train station, or sometimes took the bus home, depending on where she was. In winter, migrating birds had left for warmer lands in Africa. There was no birdsong except for the male blackbird's, a deep and melancholy sound as if he too felt alone in the winter. He did, the females had gone south. Irawati walked from one circle of lamplight to the next, disconcerted by how bitterly cold it was, and growing colder every day. That first winter she was tempted to go straight to bed when she got home, it seemed the right thing to do. But she soon got used to it, that it wasn't the night, but rather just that a part of the day was dark. She even went to the park, and a few times to cafes in the early evening, with Oma, or other students who were by then friends, to sit at the sidewalk tables and watch people.

It was not as it was in the summer, when organ grinders could be heard sometimes, playing their happy-sad tunes as people chatted and laughed, smoked and drank, read their books and papers, or *Die Schönheit*, the beauty magazine. Now, they were in long thick coats, in gloves and boots and all manner of hats and scarves, women and men in furs, their breath appearing in small clouds to hang briefly on the cold air. She began to enjoy the subtle and not so subtle changes of this season: the muted sounds, the ice flowers on her window panes, even the bare trees, the frozen river and the snow itself. She wondered how it was for those who would always have this season, for whom it was normal. She wondered how she would feel about it if it wasn't an anomaly in her own life. Children were apparently not as affected by the cold as adults. They did things that small children back home could never do—throw snowballs, pull each other around on pieces of cardboard or homemade sleds on the ice, and make snowmen. In December, there were Christmas markets with their smell of hot spiced wine, and food stalls and pretty lights, and it was odd to her, but common to see people dragging, or hauling large trees in trucks.

Before Christmas Day, Irawati took the train to Leipzig. She would not be returning to Berlin for a month.

In 1920, barely two years after the end of the Great War, Dinkar Karve had arrived in Germany much the same way Irawati had. By passenger steamship, for higher education. He had stayed four years in Germany. He had clearly enjoyed his time in the country, he talked about it fondly, and he kept in touch with friends he had made there. Photographs of him from his German years show him in many family gatherings. Festive meals, picnics and outings, even trips far from the places where he was studying, such as The Bodensee (Lake

Constance,) far in the south, on the border between Germany and Switzerland. He had stayed first in Berlin, with Oma, to learn German, and then in Leipzig, where he did his PhD in chemistry, at the Leipzig University. There he stayed with the lovely, and loving, and very large, Seebass family. Herr and Frau Seebass—Karl and Maria—had five sons and four daughters, who all lived with them in a large house. Dinu had enough money in his possession to meet all of his daily needs for the entirety of his stay there, or so he believed. The money, as a citizen of the British Empire, was in pounds sterling, and, as was normal, he converted all of his pounds to Reichsmark. But, as the Weimar Republic struggled to pay its war reparations debt, the value of money steadily declined, and by 1923, Dinu would have been destitute, and left with no choice but to return home. The Seebass family was by then his German family. They fed and took care of him till he had his degree, never wanting anything in return. They had naturally stayed in touch, so it was with great joy that they took the news of Irawati's arrival in Berlin. They told Dinu that she must stay with them during her holidays—all her holidays.

Any apprehension Irawati might have felt dissipated within seconds of arriving at their house. She was hugged and kissed, whether she liked it or not, by every member of that large family. The old parents, the sons, the daughters, the daughters-in-law, and children who were new additions since Dinu's time there, and even visiting cousins—they all lined up and welcomed her with kisses. She didn't dislike it, but it was strange, to have such intimate contact with complete strangers. By the end of that first visit, she became completely accustomed to the kissing, and she too, like Dinu, became a member of the Seebass family. They, like Oma, began their relationship on a positive note. They already expected to love her because she was the wife of their 'Dinu'. She went back to Leipzig on all the festive holidays. It was nice to get away from Berlin and her studies, but it was genuinely good to be surrounded by people whose company she enjoyed, and who all clearly enjoyed hers and looked forward to her arrival with as much pleasure as she did, in spite of all the kissing.

Irawati was particularly drawn to Ria, the eldest Seebass son's wife, possibly because they were around the same age. Their friendship made her look forward to her Leipzig visits even more. After that first Christmas, it had been some time before she could visit again. Ria was pregnant, and, when Irawati finally went for a proper long stay, Ria had given birth to a baby boy. He was a delightful plump creature, and Irawati was thrilled and loved him at once. She snatched him from Ria, cuddled him and held him close.

'Ria, I could eat him up, he's so lovely,' she said, and covered his little pink face with kisses. She became aware that the family were staring at her in consternation, and Ria laughed as she took the child back and laid him in his cot. After dinner, Irawati walked with Ria in the grounds and asked about the incident. Ria said gently, 'Iru my dear, it's alright with us, but you must never kiss little babies like that.' Irawati was thoroughly confused. With all the kissing that went on between random adults, she couldn't kiss a perfectly kissable baby?

'Babies have weak immune systems,' Ria explained. 'They could get very sick from the germs we adults carry, you know. He could get a cold, or worse. I hope you don't mind me telling you.' To prove she was not hurt or angry, Irawati kissed Ria, and they laughed.

Irawati took this incident, characteristically, as a lesson. It was the opposite back home. There you could kiss all the babies you liked, but kissing between adults was not ever a subject of conversation. One day when she was visiting Oma, the old lady had actually burst into tears saying, 'I know I disgust you, it must be because you are high caste, isn't it so?' Irawati had been stunned to discover that she had been unconsciously wiping her cheek whenever Oma kissed her. She had been the one laughing that day, and apologising for her inadvertent gesture. It was from being unused to being kissed, she explained.

'Do you wipe your face when your mother kisses you too?' Oma had asked her, unbelievingly.

'Oma,' Irawati said, 'Unlike you, my mother would not ever kiss a grown woman, not even her own daughter!' They had both laughed at that. Cultures are so different, Irawati thought, and so are their ways of showing affection and love.[10]

After the idyllic weeks in Leipzig, the warmth and the meals, and sweets and festivities, surrounded by a family that treated her as one of their own, Berlin looked bleak and felt terribly cold. It was a beautiful but dreadful sight when ice blocks formed on the Spree and the canals and lakes all froze over. It seemed the long part of the winter that everyone had warned her about had now begun. With the holidays behind them, there was nothing to sustain them but the hope of an early spring—which, if they were fortunate, would arrive in March.

Life went on as usual, cold or not, dark or not—the work on her PhD project, her classes. Day upon day upon day. One afternoon she finished her work for the day and went to the window and sat there on a chair, staring at the leafless tree outside. She just wanted to gather herself before tackling the dark and cold and strangers that she would encounter on her way home. She had no idea how long she had been sitting there when she felt a hand on her shoulder. She turned and saw Professor Fischer standing behind her, an expression on his face that she had never seen before: concern, empathy, as if she were his daughter. She did not realise that her face was wet from the tears still streaming from her eyes.

'The leaves will be back soon,' he said, 'the winter is over.'

Irawati was at once comforted and confused. How could this man, so unlike her in every way, know what she was feeling, and how could he show such a side of himself to her, she wondered. He stood there for a moment, looking at the stoic linden, and then quietly left.

As she walked down the staircase that she was now used to, she thought about that first winter, the first time it snowed and how that was for her, the soundless precipitation, something she could not even have imagined, coming from the land of monsoons, of thunderous rain, pittering rain, battering hail—where even the gentlest rainfall made a sound when it touched a solid surface. Snow fell that night, enveloping the sounds of the city, and all night there was a glow inside her room. And the next day the snow was in a different, a treacherous form. She had slipped and fallen on the unseen ice beside the pavement and had broken her arm. When she had been x-rayed and plastered at the Charité hospital she went to see Eugen Fischer. She was feeling alone, feeling like a small unwanted and lost stranger in the metropolis of Berlin, and a broken one. He had been kind and reassuring, and given her work that she could do with her one good arm. That had made her feel useful, and that made her forget how poor she felt. He was a strange man, she thought. She was still a stranger in this city, and she had been grateful to him then.

~

New Orleans Honky-Tonk spilled out from the open doors and windows of the enormous restaurant that had been rented for their year-end party. The sound of revellers shouting and laughing could be heard for at least a block. Not that this was unusual or much of a spectacle on any Berlin evening, drinking and dancing was a normal matter, every day of the week. Irawati noticed a man in a peculiar bulbous hat leaned up against a lamppost, smoking a cigarette. He watched as the crowd of people outside were slowly accommodated into the restaurant. He had a pile of cigarette stubs at his feet, and he seemed to be in an ill mood. He made eye contact with her and shook his head disapprovingly. Irawati felt she understood the generally dour spirit of the native Berliner. It reminded her of the attitude of the Punekar, and she was quite at home with it. Berlin bus drivers were as likely to refuse to give out information; Berlin shop owners were as likely to make you feel you were imposing on their time by shopping at their establishment; and old Berlin ladies were just as likely to teach you the local manners, as were all their Pune counterparts. But it was also true of Berliners that they would go out of their way to take you to an address if you were lost and asked for directions.

'Nofretete,' the smoking man said to her with a sudden wide smile, bringing her out of her reverie. She had heard that one before. She smiled back at him, and then moved with the crowd as it trickled through the doors. It was raucous inside. Beer had already been consumed in large amounts, people were singing with all their might, they were not yet dancing on the tables, but she knew that was coming, and in the melee, students and teachers were indistinguishable from each other in their revelry. Irawati stood against a wall with a glass of Apfel-Schorle in her hand. She thought about what the man outside had said. It was not the first time someone had compared her to that other, more famous, Berlin native since 1920. They called her 'Noff-ruh-tay-tuh'. It became a sort of compliment, because she was just exotic enough, she supposed. Sometimes she was asked if she was a Pashtoon lady from Afghanistan, by people who knew a bit better than those who likened her to the newly acquired bust of Nefertiti.[11] Though she herself wasn't dark enough or different enough to alarm anyone's sensibilities, they knew she was foreign, perhaps because of her sarees, which most people found exotic, even if they said they were elegant.

The queen was a new and amazing arrival in the city, and not only that, she too, like Irawati, was installed in Dahlem. Irawati and Nefertiti, Oriental and exotic, it seemed acceptable for people to compare them.

The face of Nefertiti was two mirrored halves, whether the work of the artist or the god who made the woman he rendered in limestone and paint. What did they know, these Germans, about symmetry, about asymmetry. Asymmetry was normal, and the Nile Queen, in her perfection, was a singularity. What did Eugen Fischer know about symmetry, or was it that he knew, and was so jealous of it that he found a way to punish them, Irawati and Nefertiti?

Fischer had assigned her to prove his hypothesis. He had instructed her to '1) determine if there exist differences in the [skull's] right-side and left-side asymmetry, and 2) if differences in the frequency of the asymmetry of different races occur, especially in the case of European and other races.'[12] She had done the work, precisely and meticulously. She had measured the skulls she was supposed to measure. The European, the African, the Papua New Guinean, the Melanesian. One hundred and forty-nine head bones had answered her question. They had spoken to her from the past, they had sent their message, through her and her calculations, to her present.

Irawati had done what no one else, in the entire history of the KWI-A had done. She had stated that she could not observe any correlation between racial differences and the measured skull asymmetries. Asymmetry in the human skull was normal—independent of which 'race' that skull was supposed to represent. That asymmetry did not point to any racial superiority or inferiority in the owner of said skull, and not to the 'race' the owner of the skull belonged to either. Nor did she stop there. She put forward another hypothesis for skull asymmetry, asymmetry in the spinal column—a product, not of heredity or race, but a physical characteristic that could be a product of the environment, and not an inherited, born-with characteristic. She had contradicted Fischer's hypotheses, of course, but also the theories of that institute and the mainstream theories of the time to boot.

Irawati's research disproved her *Doktorvater's* theory that European skulls would be found asymmetrical because of their superior powers of logic and reasoning, and non-European skulls would be, for obvious reasons, symmetrical.

Eugen Fisher had not been pleased, let alone proud of his student. He had not failed her outright, but he had given her the lowest possible grade: *Doneux,* Latin for suitable, or sufficient. He had alluded to her non-native, German speaking skills as being a possible reason. Her foreignness. Irawati thought this was laughable. What would Oma say, she thought, when Irawati told her, in perfect German, that her German had been judged inadequate. Her friends and colleagues had laughed. They had all joked about it. In German. Still, Irawati was relieved. She would have her degree after all. She would soon be Dr Irawati Karve. Soon, and forever.

If symmetry is a form of perfection, Nefertiti's symmetrical head, and her symmetrical skull, were really just perfection then. And Eugen Fischer would have to live with that. A black African woman, who had been dead for longer than time. The most beautiful woman in Berlin, they said. Irawati smiled once more.

One of her fellow students, a young man who had been singing, dancing and drinking vigorously, and kissing everyone in the room in a fit of high sentimentality, came right up to Irawati, and before she could react or say anything, took her face in his hands and kissed her loudly on both cheeks. She was taken aback, offended, and shocked all at once. She wiped her face with the end of her saree, and shook her head disapprovingly, but he just laughed and moved on to his next victim.

The party was just beginning. She was glad she would be home again, not soon, but soon enough.

~

One evening after a hurried walk from the station through the endless cold that went deeper and deeper into her core, Irawati pushed open one side of the heavy glass and wood double doors to the entrance of Kaiserdamm 88. In the welcome warmth, she heard voices as she walked down the maroon and green floral-tiled passage; it sounded more heated than usual chatter. The apartments housed several students, and they would sometimes gather on the stairs, away from the cold outside, smoking and talking. When she came around the corner to go up the stairs, she saw four or five young men, angry and all talking at once, belligerently, but not touching each other. It was a political disagreement. They quietened down when they saw her, and the one who seemed to be at the receiving end of the shouting followed her up the stairs. She knew him slightly, they had talked sometimes, and once they had walked the short distance from the U-Bahn together. All the students lived on the floor above her. She had heard arguments before, so she didn't think much of it. She had a letter from Dinu to read.

The time Irawati would be in Germany was now less than the time she had been there. She thought about how it would be being back home, among her family and friends, what her new job would be. She would see Dinu again. Although her father-in-law had never relented about his decision to not support her in her education abroad, she had good news on another front. Her own father too, who had thought she was already educated enough when she passed the fourth year of elementary school, had flatly refused to support this PhD foolishness, let alone being away from her new husband in a foreign country that was not England. Dinu wrote that Mr Karmarkar had had a turnaround. Irawati was, after all, his favourite child, and his only daughter. He would pay for Dinu to travel to Germany and have a holiday with his still new wife, and bring her home to start their married life together. Iru got under the fluffy covers into the freezing cold bed, and this night she didn't mind the cold, nor the huge square pillow that she would never get used to no matter how long she lived there. Falling asleep with this happy news, she had no inkling of what awaited her the next morning. She would never forget what would transpire, at Kaiserdamm 88, Berlin, 1929. It would take on a different meaning, later in her life, decades later. In hindsight, it was one among twenty million markers on a cruel and bloody road.

The wood bannister slid under Irawati's palm as if it was

moving rather than she, slipping backward into the past, the past that she would long for after that day, in the way of all of us who wish for the thing that happened to go back into un-happening. She knew, before she began that hurried descent, she knew, as she neared the shock, the sadness, the fear, the blood and death that would confront her, she knew, that if she went there, she would be forever changed. She knew, but it was already too late, it is always too late. We go where we have already been, again and again, a snake eating its tail; we, small, helpless, swallowed and spat out, swallowed and spat out, incapable of changing the beginning, the end, the middle, feeling everything. All we can do is feel it, and she soon would.

Irawati had come too fast out of the building, and not expecting the crowd to be so close to the entrance, unable to stop herself, had run into a man standing by the body. He almost fell, and recovered himself, and let her get to the front to look. There were so many people there, but it was so very quiet. No one spoke. Silence had fallen, had already taken over. Someone had covered the boy in an old bedsheet. Embroidered green vines trailed over the mounds and valleys of his ever-unmoving body, a row of neat stitches on an old rip in the sheet ran over the knuckles of his hand. Irawati looked up, to the building, to the window. She saw indistinct white faces turned to her. She shivered and wrapped her arms tight around herself, and still looking up, imagined they knew who and what she was. She looked down then, at the sheet fluttering at the edges of the boy's remains, sticking in the viscosity of his life-juices. Through the urgent deafening beat of her horrified heart, she found something else of his, something precious, in her memory. Perhaps he had known, what was to come. Perhaps he knew too, that it was too late.

And as he had passed her on the stairs, that evening before, he had left that with her, to remember him by: his smile.

~

Oma had made a cake for Irawati, a thick high slice sat on a gold-rimmed china plate in front of her. Oma poured coffee for them both.

'Here,' she said, handing Irawati the flower-patterned, gold-rimmed cup and its matching saucer. Irawati held it, not drinking it, feeling the warmth on her hand. She had said nothing to Oma since she had arrived.

'My dear, is something wrong?' Oma asked her.

'Wrong? That young man, that boy, he was—thrown out of the window, murdered, and we—how can we sit here and eat cake and drink coffee as if—as if—' The cup began to rattle on the saucer and she put it on the table. 'My God, do you have no heart?' Irawati blurted out, too loudly, and regretted it immediately. Before she could apologise, Oma set her fork down.

'Iru, eat the cake, drink your coffee. There is nothing to say about that, nothing. You understand.'

Irawati had understood. She was shocked, but not surprised. Everyone had turned their eyes and faces from what had happened, and what was happening. They were not pretending, they were genuinely closing themselves off to it all, they were protecting their own hearts and minds, and perhaps, by doing so, their own skins. This young man, this Jewish student, would be forgotten then, intentionally and carefully. *She* would have to remember him, all by herself. She thought the trauma of the incident would not allow her to remember, she thought her mind would fight to forget.

The chemistry of fear had distorted her smell and sight, the recollection of what she saw had a hallucinatory, dream quality to it, but she remembered. She remembered the window light change for an instant before that sound. She wondered how it was that she had recognised a sound that she had never heard before: flesh and bone ending in concrete. She began to shake. She thought she must be shell-shocked, like those broken soldiers begging all over Berlin. Those incomplete men, missing limbs, fingers, eyes, incomplete, inside and out, war-beggars in a beggared country. This was not her country, but she felt a strange tightness in her heart for it. Defeated, cornered, hounded, what would become of it? The despair was not on the periphery, not at the edges of the eye, it was right there, you had to turn away from it, to hide it from your sight.

'Turn a blind eye,' she thought, 'both eyes blind, both ears deaf, and the mouth mute. And then what.'

What would come, after Irawati left that city with Dinkar, is well documented now. She had seen the best of Germany, and the worst. She packed her new tools to take home with her—her craniophor, the eye-colour charts, the skin and hair colour charts, the anthropometer—the instruments that would measure human difference. She and Dinkar left by train, to travel west through Europe before they took a steamship home.

Irawati would never return to Berlin.

Part Two

5

Pardesh

Flowing south from Mandalay, the great Irrawaddy River turns sharply west at the city of Irawati's birth. It makes a wide curve there, and then flows down through lower Burma (now Myanmar) to Rangoon, spreading into a wide delta before emptying into the Andaman Sea. This waterway is the road to Mandalay. Irawati was born there, in 1905, in Myingyan, a city at the river's edge. Two decades before, in 1886, the British had repulsed massive attacks on its garrisons, survived raging fevers among the troops, and finally crushed a bitter revolt in Myingyan and the entire province of Mandalay, as they had in many parts of British Burma and India. So, when she was born, Irawati was born a British subject.

In the Indian tradition of giving girls the names of rivers, her father, Ganesh Hari Karmarkar, gave her the name Irawati, though no girl had ever been named for that particular river before. He might have known that his daughter, born after his four sons, needed a name that signalled her uniqueness to the world.

Ganesh Karmarkar himself was born in Paud, in Maharashtra. He was an enterprising young man with ambition, and when opportunity came his way, he found a way to grasp it. He applied for a job at the British Cotton Company, in Burma. When he told this story to his children years later, he recalled that as he sat outside the office of the administrator who would interview him, he began to think that there was a better than good chance he would not get the job. There were several young men seated on the long wooden benches, waiting along with him. They seemed to him somehow more confident than himself, possibly because they were qualified for the job. He knew for certain that they were better qualified than he was. The preferred candidate was an engineer, which he was not, or required at least some knowledge and experience in the management of factories, and he had neither.

Ganesh waited. Every ten or fifteen minutes, a man would come out of the office after his interview, the khaki uniformed peon would go into the office, come out, call a name, and the next person would go in. Ganesh noticed that all the hopefuls were shorter, and also darker-skinned than himself. It was only the idle observation of a wandering mind. When, after a wait of almost two hours, his name was finally called, he was startled. He picked up the mostly empty leather briefcase he had brought along to convey seriousness, and went into the office. The Englishman behind the big wooden desk did not look up as he came in.

'Mr Harry Karmarkar?' he said, unaware and unconcerned that he was hopelessly mangling the name, and continued without waiting for an answer or looking up for a nod, 'yes, so, you are able to relocate yourself to Myingyan, then?'

'Yes, certainly,' Ganesh said, and then the Englishman looked up sharply. He gazed at Ganesh and then said with a big smile, 'You are quite the fellow' and nodded for Ganesh to sit down.

'Get your looks from your mother?' he asked, and Ganesh was momentarily confused, and then he understood. The man had assumed Ganesh's mother was English, because of his height and fair skin, and his clear and very large light grey eyes that were not uncommon in his Chitpavan Brahmin community.

'Yes,' Ganesh said, nodding and smiling, 'I do have my mother's eyes.'

They talked for some time about the weather in Burma, and then the health of Viceroy Lord Curzon and of the Queen. Nothing at all was said about either the job or his experience, and Ganesh began to feel sure that the interview was a failure for him, when the Englishman asked him if he would like some tea.

'You will be ready to leave by the end of this month?' he asked, and Ganesh was at once relieved and a little bit guilty. When he was back home, he explained to his wife, Bhagirathi, that he himself had not so much lied as allowed the Englishman to believe that he was unlike all the other interviewees.

'What do you mean,' she asked, not understanding.

'He thought I was Anglo,' Ganesh said laughing, 'and I didn't say I wasn't.' And then, thinking about it, he said, 'But maybe that's not what happened. Maybe he just thought I was the right candidate for the job. Or, he just liked me.'

Ganesh knew, though, what had really happened. He had not divested the man of his misinterpretation. He knew it was his height, his skin, his eyes, and perhaps his gumption, that had got him that job.

~

As they waited to board the train, Bhagirathi pulled her saree tight across herself and tucked it into her waist. This way it would not flap about behind her or get in her way as she navigated the crowds on the platform, or obstruct her arms when she carried the two cloth bags, in which she had a silver mango-shaped box with her kunku, the jewellery that she had received from her parents and her in-laws on her marriage to Ganesh, her green wedding saree, and a few other precious things. These she had not packed into the large trunks with their luggage. When the train left the station and the city limits, it also left the limits of Bhagirathi's known world. Everything she saw from then on as they were carried across the broadest part of the subcontinent was new to her. Landscapes she had never seen, huge rivers and wide plains in the distance, strange trees and shrubs closer to the tracks, and the people who got on and off the train—even they looked different from anyone she had ever seen. As they went further east, there were men, women and children with strange eyes and smooth faces and smooth hair, all wearing shirts made of pretty woven cloth. They all wore loose lower garments that could only be called pants, even the women. There were many British soldiers and civilians, some of them were with them the entire journey. She lost track of time and space, as the train rattled and vibrated for days and days. And as they went further and further away from anything familiar, and familiar-looking people were replaced by real strangers, she could no longer understand what anyone around her was saying. There was only her husband to talk to, and she slowly began to understand that now, aside from him, she was very much alone.

Although it wasn't as if she had any choice in the matter, she was not afraid or timid. She arrived in Myingyan, to her an enormous metropolis, but actually a town of less than twenty thousand. There was a railway station that brought travellers and soldiers passing through, and sometimes British officials keeping an eye on this outpost of the empire. The port of Myingyan on the Irrawaddy was quite busy, river traffic stopped there on its way north and south. There were a few British soldiers and administrators stationed there, and a few other British citizens from various parts of India, there was the cotton mill of which her husband was the manager, and there was the Irrawaddy. They were quite well off, but there was really nothing much for her to do. The social life was closed to her, because she spoke neither English nor Burmese, nor the languages the other Indians spoke.

She kept house, she experimented with cooking, she made pickles, and she explored. In the evenings, when they had eaten the dinner that she had cooked with the strange local vegetables, Ganesh would sit with his wife and teach her to read and write. She had never been to school. Not only did he teach her to read and write Marathi, he taught her English as well, by reading the novels of Somerset Maugham aloud to her. And he taught her basic numbers and accounting.

While she was perfecting her English and arithmetic, the couple was growing their family. They had many children. Her pregnancies were not always easy. In fact, the trauma of some was so deep that she erased all memory of it, and when asked later in her life, she could not recall how many children she had actually carried and lost. Some she lost and some survived, but one thing was true: the living and the dead, they were all male children. By 1905, the couple had four living sons between the ages of five and sixteen. And that year, when they thought their life was as it was going to be, they found she was, once again, with child. This time, though, was completely different. On December 15, 1905, Ganesh Hari Karmarkar and his wife were thrilled and joyful at the birth of their youngest child: their first, and only, daughter.

Ganesh Karmarkar, father of four sons named Shankar, Prabhakar, Mahesh, and Hemant, not extraordinary names by any stretch, was inspired by this thoroughly unexpected turn of events. He gave his daughter, at least as far as he knew, a name that was hers alone. What he did not know was that this name, that was at once unique and lovely, and that carried the history of her birth and the weight of singularity within it, was one that she would live up to, whether her father liked it or not.

Right from the moment Irawati was born, she was the most precious thing in the world to not just her parents, but all of her four brothers. She was small and transparent and delicate to them, and needed to be watched over and looked after at every moment. She was given whatever she wanted, and loved as much as she wanted and more. She was a princess, and her father, and brothers, and her mother, doted on her in ways that gave new meaning to that word.

Life in Myingyan was idyllic for Irawati. They were wealthy by the time she came along, and her father was as high up as a person who was not altogether white could get in the British Cotton Company administration. Ganesh Karmarkar was quite pleased with his life too, and his sons, and his wife, who could read and write, and keep accounts for the family, and, thanks to his teaching, speak English. All was well with the Karmarkar family, and with Irawati, the child with the name of the river.

What then, in the midst of all this contentment, could have made him decide one day, to send their little Irawati, all of six years old, to a boarding school—the Huzurpaga School for Girls—thousands of miles away, in Pune?

Many of the Englishmen working in the colonies sent their school-aged children back to Britain to be educated. Some left their wives at home too, or with their parents or in-laws, and the children went to day schools. Those who could afford it sent the children to boarding schools. Not many children went to local schools in the colonies, particularly in smaller places where the schooling language was not English, and particularly when the children were past elementary school age.

'This is what my colleagues do,' Ganesh explained to his wife and sons, and to Irawati, who could not possibly have understood what this meant. 'All their children are sent home for their education.'

Home for Irawati had always been their house in Myingyan. The impressive two-storey house sat high on a hill. It was a large, spacious house, even for their growing family. There was no stone or brick in its construction at all. It had huge teak columns and wood and bamboo walls, even the roof was made from wooden slats attached to wooden crossbeams. The house swayed in the frequent rainstorms, and complained and rattled when there was an occasional earthquake, but it was never damaged in the slightest, nor was it in any danger of falling. When the Irrawaddy River was in flood, Irawati could see it from the windows of the upper floor. She had never left Burma, so she had never seen Pune, this place that her father called 'home' and where he was sending her.

In the school holidays of 1912, when Irawati was seven years old, she came back to Myingyan once. Her father was in India for work, and on impulse, decided to bring her back with him. The journey to Myingyan was four days long, sometimes more. But even as a young girl, Irawati loved to travel. It was three days by train, on a large wooden bench in the second class compartment. During the daytime, she watched wonderful sights of nature and towns that flowed like a movie reel. At night, the constant clack-clack of the carriages on the tracks took her into a delicious sleep. When they reached the end of that part of the journey, they embarked on the next—three days on the Bay of Bengal in a boat to Rangoon. They spent a few days in that city, and finally boarded a train home to Myingyan. Through dense teak forests, a wall of identical large leafed trees, the odour of decaying foliage in the air, she found this part of the journey monotonous, and it was a relief when they finally emerged from the forest and arrived at Myingyan station.

Irawati took great pleasure in renewing her acquaintance with this place she had known so well, her only home until she had been sent away. The house, the Irrawaddy, of course her mother, who was deeply happy to have her daughter home. For Irawati, the best surprise of all was Sadashiv: a brand new beautiful baby brother.

When days turned to weeks and weeks to months, the newness of the old place palled, the little brother, though utterly delightful, was just too little, her two older brothers who had been her playfellows were away in India. She soon became bored. She missed her friends and her boarding school, and she began to beg her parents to send her back to Huzurpaga. Then Ganesh Karmarkar needed to return to India, and, to her immense relief, she left Myingyan once again, this time happily, even though she knew her mother wept to see her go.

When Irawati was gone, Bhagirathi saw that the cook had placed a lump of jaggery in front of the Krishna statue in their home altar. When she asked him about it, he said Iru-tai had asked him to. He said that Irawati had prayed to Krishna every day to send her back to India, and when he did, the cook was to thank him for her, with jaggery. Tears began to flow from Bhagirathi's eyes, but she knew it was the way of children to leave. And the lot of mothers left behind to weep.

6

River Crossing

The winter sunshine slanted through the huge gulmohar tree and lit up the very small figure sitting on the stone bench below it. The child looked even smaller because the light wrapped around her. The man stopped and spoke to her.

'Are you waiting for your parents?' he asked gruffly, from under his impressive, and though she did not know it then, legendary whiskers.

'I live here,' she said, in a clear voice, 'I'm just sitting here because the children are making too much noise inside.'

'Is that so,' the man said smiling, 'were they disturbing your reading?'

She nodded.

'Well, then, I won't disturb you either,' he said, and walked away. Irawati went back to her book, unaware that this man would, arguably, be among the most influential in her life.

The man of the moustaches was R.P. Paranjpye.

A Wrangler is a person who graduates first class in mathematics at Cambridge University. A Senior Wrangler stands at the top of the class in the final mathematics examination. R.P. Paranjpye became Wrangler Paranjpye at

Saint John's College of the University of Cambridge in 1899. He was the first Indian to do so. Wrangler Paranjpye, or R.P. as he was widely and affectionately known, was the principal of Fergusson College in Pune. He was deeply respected, but also, universally loved by all who knew him, including his colleagues, his students, and his friends and family. He was the husband of 'Saitai', and the father of Shakuntala, who was Irawati's classmate, and friend.

One weekend, Shakuntala brought her friend Irawati, and a gaggle of other classmates home with her. All of them ran around in the compound playing some hectic game, and when they were tired and thirsty, they came into the kitchen, where Shakuntala's mother was picking through rice. Each girl gulped down a tumbler of water from the matka, and immediately went out again. The last girl to drink water, a shy, pale girl with light eyes, stood there for a minute after she was done drinking, and smiled at her.

'You can call me Saitai,' Mrs Paranjpye said, 'And what is your name?'

'Irawati.'

'Irawati? What an unusual name. What does it mean?'

Irawati told her what it meant, and where it was from, and was soon sitting down and helping pick through the rice for little stones and other impurities. She felt very comfortable beside this lady, a feeling of warmth came over her. Perhaps she had been unaware of having missed the feeling, or perhaps, she had just put it aside as something to deal with another time, and it had come upon her unawares. Whatever the reason, Irawati felt a sense of belonging in Mrs Paranjpye's—Saitai's—presence. They sat like that for some time, talking and laughing. Suddenly Saitai said to her, 'Would you like to come and live here with me?' and Irawati, without knowing why, without thinking about it, replied, 'Yes. I would.'

Saitai told her husband.

'I will make inquiries about this matter,' he said. True to his word, but also because his wife pestered him about it, R.P. Paranjpye made the promised inquiries. Irawati Karmarkar was, the principal of Huzurpaga School for Girls informed him, the child of parents who lived in Burma. R.P. was gruff and tough, a man's man in many ways. But those who knew him knew he was a tender-hearted person. Although he conveyed his emotions as outrage, his reasons for wanting Irawati to come into his home were different from his wife's. He could not bear the thought of this small, pale, delicate child, from his own Chitpavan Brahmin community, living in the school like an orphan, among people who no doubt looked after her, but who were after all, staff and paid employees. For this little girl, who had a family, and yet had to live outside family life as if she had no one in the world was utterly unacceptable, even painful for him. It was one thing to go there as a day scholar. But to live there, in a building that used to be the stables of the Peshwa rulers of Maharashtra, added another layer of unacceptability to the situation.

'She is very small and alone. I cannot imagine how it must be to live without a family, to have no meals together with your mother and father and siblings, to sleep with a group of strangers, to have no one to look at you with love.'

The Wrangler did not need his wife to push him to do what had to be done. He demanded that the child be sent to his home as soon as possible. He assured the principal of the school that he would contact the parents and let them know, and everything would be alright. The principal was not about to go against the wishes of this highly respected and important man in Pune, who was also the principal of Fergusson College, which was just one among many of his illustrious posts. The Wrangler informed Ganesh and Bhagirathi Karmarkar,

Irawati's parents, of his decision. They did not object to this new arrangement, or, more likely, they were not given the choice. It might have seemed prudent, Myingyan being so far from Pune, to acquiesce to the wishes of a man even they knew by his reputation. The only change Ganesh Karmarkar made was that he began to send the school boarding money to the Paranjpye house, because that, to him, was the correct thing to do.

This entire incident, though it is a matter of history now, was without doubt peculiar in many ways. Why did Saitai and her husband pick this particular child from among all the girls in the school to bring home with them? Why did Irawati's father allow them, strangers, to take his daughter home? The answers to these questions are lost in time. Be what they may, Saitai took to Irawati. Her childlike insistence that Irawati must live with them combined with the reputation and respect her husband commanded began another chapter in Irawati's young life.

Not long after the conversation in the kitchen, Irawati, aged seven, went from Huzurpaga Girls' High School where she was a child among other children and a ward of adult strangers, to live with the Paranjpye family on the other side of Pune, on the other side of the Mutha river.

It is not at all a fantastic or preposterous thing to say that this river crossing was not merely a geographical one. Irawati, that little girl from Myingyan, Burma, had just stepped onto the road that she would walk on for the rest of her life.

~

The Paranjpye house was surrounded by trees young and old that insulated the walls in the dry heat of Pune's endless summers. The house had balconies upstairs and verandas downstairs, large cool, dark rooms with shelves full of books. Cats were a most important part of the Paranjpye household, they came and went as they pleased. The house shared the grounds of the Fergusson College campus, with its Gothic basalt stone main building, and all the gravity of an academic institution. Professors, students, and other members of the academy, therefore, also came and went as they pleased.

In Shakuntala, Irawati had a sister, after living her life with four brothers. Iru and Shaku. They went to school together, they came home together, they ate together, they did their homework together. They were inseparable, and though there were unavoidable sisterly spats, they adored each other. As they grew older, there were other feelings beneath the surface, and unspoken rivalries too.

Mrs Paranjpye and Irawati became close, they had been drawn to each other from the moment they met, and Saitai, as she was called by all except her own daughter, became as a second mother for Irawati. Irawati called R.P. Paranjpye Appa, and he became her second father, and so much more, but that took time. At first, he terrified her. A man with a fascinating moustache and booming voice was one thing in a single meeting and a short conversation one evening. It was quite another thing for a child to live with him in his household, where he was the master, and his big laugh and gruff voice reigned. Appa Paranjpye was an imposing man, particularly to a small girl like Irawati. Shakuntala and Saitai, his daughter and wife, were used to him. Even though Shakuntala got more than Irawati did in terms of 'discipline'—corporal punishment in the form of beatings—Shakuntala, because she was not afraid of anyone or anything, was also not afraid of her father. To Saitai, he never said an unkind word, or ever raised his voice to her, let alone his hand. If he was provoked by her in any way, he would resort to a quote from Jane Austen. His favourite was Mister Bennet from *Pride and Prejudice.* Bennet, father to five girls and husband to a wife prone to faintings and tremblings of all kinds, was a person Appa Paranjpye identified with. He, in his own mind, was the beleaguered Mister Bennet, beset by feminine silliness and childishness from all sides. As Irawati grew older, she understood that there was much more that her dear Appa was covering up with the dry humour he borrowed from Mister Bennet.

Saitai, according to Irawati, was a sweet-natured and gentle woman, with an almost naïvely generous spirit who was nothing but kind to Irawati. It was with her, in their kitchen, that Irawati and Shakuntala learned to cook. Not just them, but any and all children who frequented the house, be they boys or girls, helped in the kitchen. Picking over rice, shelling beans and peas, and, as they got older, wielding knives and experimenting with cooking. By the time Irawati and Shakuntala were running their own kitchens, they had learned all the basics of Maharashtrian food. Poli, rice, sour daal, all kinds of vegetable curries, and sabudana khichadi, they could make it all.

There were rituals in the Paranjpye household. Not religious ones, because this was an atheist family for generations, but rituals nevertheless, that were passed down to the generations yet to come. One such was reading aloud to each other. Many a classic was easily and enjoyably learned by the whole family together. Appa would assign a character for each of them to read, and they would read aloud in the evening or after dinner, much like the characters from Victorian England. Dickens, Goldsmith, even Shakespeare was put behind them, an education that happened without anyone noticing.

Appa would shave himself every morning at a mirror by his bedroom window. Iru and Shaku were to sit behind him where he could keep a stern eye on them as he shaved, and a stern ear too, on their diction, as they took turns to read. Among all of the authors that Appa loved and admired, Jane Austen reigned supreme. They read *Pride and Prejudice*, of course, not just once, but many times, usually followed by *Mansfield Park*. He would correct their pronunciations as they read, between stropping his straight razor, swishing his pig bristle brush on a shaving bar, lathering up his face, and then, to Irawati's fascination, scraping the stubble off his face, carefully, around his marvellous moustache. All the while the girls took turns to read. And along with ascribing the role of Mister Bennet to himself and that of the rather silly and hypochondriac Mrs Bennet to his own wife Saitai, which no doubt stung her, Shaku was the smart and mouthy Elizabeth Bennet, and Irawati herself was Fanny Price, the heroine of Mansfield Park.

There was another lady who lived in that house, to whom R.P. assigned the role of Mrs Norris from *Mansfield Park*. This was one person Irawati avoided at all costs. This lady was Saitai's mother, and Appa's mother-in-law. It was an unusual thing for a married woman's mother to live with the family, and another clue to something that Irawati understood when she was a woman herself, as things fell into place with the understanding that comes with adulthood and experience. The Mrs Norris of Mansfield Park is the sister-in-law of Sir Thomas, the master of the house. She is a widow, brought in to run the household, because Lady Thomas was, for various reasons, incapable of doing her duty. In the book, Norris spoils the children of the household while being mean to Fanny Price, who is a poor relative living with the family. The real-life Norris, Appa's mother-in-law, was a sharp-tongued woman, and her ways, Irawati felt, disturbed and upset the whole family. But she was particularly mean to Irawati, reprimanding her sometimes for good reason, but usually for no reason at all. Appa was clearly aware of these tensions in his home, but it seemed he put up with the lady in question, because though she was no doubt a Mrs Norris to everyone, and particularly to Iru's Fanny Price, she did take care of the running of the house.

Saitai was a remarkably, even unnaturally bubbly person. She had some quirks that the children simply accepted, as children do in adults—they just don't know any better, and in some instances they have nothing to compare their situation with. Even though Irawati heard the story of her lost child, who was born after Shakuntala, and who had died before he reached a year of life, she did not understand, until she was older, what effect that had had on this sweet, generous, and childlike woman.

Saitai's desire to always be surrounded by the laughter of children was perhaps why Irawati grew up in the Paranjpye home. Irawati found out that Saitai did not, would not eat unless it was in the presence of a child. If Iru-Shaku were out somewhere, or at school, she would bring the neighbour's baby, or the gardener's boy to sit with her for her meal.

Saitai liked to take the girls with her when she left the house too. She took them with her for the grocery shopping, on weekends they went to the market, and then she bought everything in sight, too many fruits and vegetables, clothes, toys, and she bought a doll for herself every month or so. She was joyful and energetic, almost frenetic. As the girls came into their teenage years, it felt like she was almost one of them, in their adolescence. And as they grew out of theirs, she was left behind, and Irawati, once close to her, began to feel a distance. Not in affection, because that would never change, but in the distance that an adult feels from a child—now she was the adult where it had once been the other way around.

Yet, there came times when Saitai's effervescence evaporated and everything about her suddenly changed. She would sit for weeks, on the far corner of her bed, almost as if to avoid the daylight; she would not speak to anyone or eat any food, she was like a ghost of herself, fallen into something that Irawati did not recognise, because she had never seen it before. She did not know, then, what it was that felled this sparkling woman, that was deeper than sadness, that was stranger than just an ordinary illness like a flu or a fever, that was clear in its path and went away when it had run its course, and for which there was no medicine.

It was during these times, when Saitai was unable to even leave her room, that 'Mrs Norris'—Saitai's mother's—role in the household became invaluable. Irawati, though she accepted it all as part of their life in the way that children do, did come to understand and knit it all together in hindsight. She was able to name what she had seen, and perhaps make sense of those manifestations of Saitai's old and endless grief. Perhaps here lay the beginnings of Irawati's remarkable ability to grasp the nuances of the unspoken, to look past the obvious and bring into focus the unseen depths of the lives of women, in the real world and in the epics. Irawati saw those shades in the lives of women in the Mahabharata: Gandhari, sent far away from her home, eager to marry a prince, only to find out that he was blind. Kunti, first in all likelihood impregnated by a sage that she was sent to serve, and then married to a man cursed to die if he had sex, and who did die in the act, but with his younger wife. Draupadi, married to not one but five men and staked, and lost, along with the kingdom, in a game of dice by the eldest, who was addicted to gambling. Irawati saw all these women, in their hardships, in their struggles, in their bravery and defiance in the teeth of everything they had to endure. Irawati herself—sent off to live away from home by her father, adopted into a home not her own; her mother, following her husband to an alien land; the child-brides who were married, and oftentimes, widowed without ever meeting their husbands; the hundreds of women Irawati encountered in her studies and field trips, even her own daughters—the ethereal, inscrutable Jai, and Gauri, bullying the neighbourhood boys, but tending lovingly to anyone who scraped a knee—Irawati admired all of them, shining and struggling within society's constraints, and saw in all of them this, their womanhood, in all its infinite variety and in all its glory.

Although Saitai was his wife, Appa himself never talked about these things to anyone let alone to Irawati. A much-loved man with countless friends and colleagues, he was nonetheless very private. In all the long years of their growing, changing relationship that was close in so many ways but never really close, Irawati had heard very little from him about those aspects of their life that were apparent, and yet unspoken. There were only two occasions, when Irawati was older, and there was a semblance of equality between her and Appa that she remembered when he had. Once, he said about his wife, 'She never really grew up, you know.' And once, 'She was ill.' That was all. In a way, these two sentences actually said everything there was to say. What else could a man like him have said, after all, about something that ran so broad and deep in their lives, and yet, that was all it was. His own grief and loss, because of course it was his too, though it did not take the physical form that Saitai's had, Irawati saw in how very much he enjoyed small children. He took the greatest delight in tiny babies, toddlers, little ones, until they were school-going boys and girls. And then he would take peculiar pleasure in minor torments, like pinching their arms, or turning them upside down, and making them scream and run away. Children never stayed away from him for long though. Later in his life, Irawati says, he shut up any mouthiness from granddaughters and grandnieces by telling them they had, after all, wet his lap when they were little.

She caught a glimpse of the real wound in him, just once, when he said to her, 'I so wanted to have a lot of children of my own.'

There was one man that he must have confided in—his closest friend and, as Irawati described him, a man who complemented Appa. This was Judge Balakram. Irawati herself admired him and enjoyed his company and his counsel. It would be Judge Balakram who nudged her toward sociology and anthropology.

Appa, or rather R.P. Paranjpye, was appointed Vice-Chancellor of Bombay University and of the Indian Women's University (1916-20), and Member of the Legislative Council of the Bombay Presidency. All these important posts, all this public prominence, all of the responsibilities and the accolades that came with his public life, were not things that Irawati and Shakuntala were really aware of, other than as new adventures. Around 1916, the Paranjpye family, along with Irawati who was very much a part of it, packed up and left the house in Pune and drove west to live in Bombay, in another large house with servants and a car and driver. Irawati remembers this part of her life as luxurious. They had vacations in Mahabaleshwar, and they ate strawberries with thick whipped cream as often as they pleased. Their readings, and their little play productions, continued. Shakuntala excelled in her studies, and she was always at the top of her class. She was her father's missing son, in a way, and he hoped that like him, she, too, would be at the top of her final mathematics exam at Saint John's College at Cambridge University. That did not happen, but she continued studying, and she did graduate from Cambridge with a mathematics degree, and he was content.

Irawati, too, continued her studies—her Bachelor's degree at Fergusson College in Pune and her Masters in Bombay University—as her own father, Ganesh Karmarkar, who was still in Myingyan, Burma, continued his objections to her pursuing her education. With the firm support of her second family, she was able to wear him down. He complained to Bhagirathi loudly and using the choicest words, that his daughter had frayed his last nerve with her argumentativeness. Bhagirathi calmly told him that Irawati must have taken after him. In spite of all his efforts, Ganesh Hari Karmarkar, who dreamt of marrying Irawati into a princely family at least, was utterly powerless to make this dream a reality. Irawati had no intention of halting her education. She was a member of the Paranjpye household now, where there was not only no objection, but an education was expected, and it was enthusiastically encouraged. Irawati found a way to make her own dream a reality, and a way to make her second father, Appa Paranjpye, proud of his own Fanny Price.

7

Childhood's End

Kartikeya, the other son of Shiva, is not one that women worship: one look at this god could mean widowhood for seven consecutive births. It was no wonder then, that no woman was ever seen at the one Kartikeya temple in the city of Pune. No woman in India wanted to be a widow, not in one lifetime, let alone seven successive reincarnations. Widows, Irawati thought, are the living dead. They were beings without control of their daily lives, or their bodies, who were nothing but domestic servants to the household, nannies for the children, and sex slaves to any male member of the family they had been married into. The women in modern day India, to her, were not far from the historical women in the Mahabharata: used, traded, controlled, treated like the possessions of their fathers, grandfathers, uncles, brothers, and then husbands and in-laws. They did what they could to make their way in the world, by fair means and foul. But widows, they were the worst off then, and still were, hundreds of years after the times of Kunti and Draupadi, Gandhari and Shakuntala and Sita.

Young widows were not uncommon in India. Girls, young enough that they were children—who sometimes had been married to men so much older than them that they could have been their grandfathers—were left widows when these men died. Sometimes the age difference was not so much, but people died of smallpox, or accidents, and so many other virulent diseases like the plague epidemic. When such calamities happened, these married children who had not yet even been sent to live with their husbands, nor even met their husbands, were suddenly told that they must have their head shaved and must not play outside but had to sit in a corner of the house. They were now widows, and their touch was polluting.

The wretchedness of widows was a topic for discussion, particularly when one gentleman came on one of his occasional visits to the house. This gentleman was Dhondo Keshav Karve. He was called Annah—older brother—by everyone, and he was R.P. Paranjpye's cousin, they shared a grandfather. They both grew up in Murud, in the Ratnagiri district on the coast of Maharashtra, which was their ancestral home. Sometime in their past Annah had brought his younger cousin, R.P., an extremely clever child, to the city of Bombay, for further studies.

Annah had seen the widow's plight, as had every other member of society. But to him, unlike most other people, their situation in society was neither acceptable, nor something that could be allowed to go on. He believed that widows should be able to live good and independent lives, and marry again if they so desired and chose to. Rather than attempting to change the way society behaves with widows, Annah Karve worked, all his life, to make choices possible for the women themselves. He felt that they must be provided with access to an education, and from that a possibility of earning an income, so they would not be at the mercy of those same people who did not have their welfare at heart. All these ideas were bad enough for Marathi society, but it got much worse for him when he put his ideas into practice. He himself had lost his wife to illness, and the pressure on him to remarry began quite soon after. He was young, he had a good job and salary, and it was normal for men to marry when their wives died. But Annah Karve declared to his mother and brother that if he were ever to marry again, it would be to a widow, and one who was of an age that was near to his own.

As it happened, a close friend of Annah Karve's had a sister who had been widowed when she was barely eight years old. She was twenty-four, about the same age as him, when they were introduced, and they both decided to marry each other. Her name was Baya.

Baya's had been a difficult life to say the least. Her given name was Godu. Her father adored her and carried her about, and his special name for her was Godubaya. After her marriage to Annah Karve she was renamed, as was the custom, as Anandi, but she continued to be called Baya by everyone. She describes in her autobiography how she was sent off to live with her in-laws, after her husband, whom she had never met, had died of smallpox when he was away from home on work. Her mother-in-law, Baya casually states, '...had in all twenty children. Out of these the first two lived, the next fourteen died, and the last three lived. (My husband, the eldest, died when he was twenty.)' This means Baya was married, at the age of six, to a man who was sixteen years her senior, and became a widow at eight. Her description of having her head shaved by the barber is harrowing, but even more harrowing is something Annah Karve found particularly despicable and disgusting: a widow had to stay shaved, and therefore had to submit to this indignity and pain not just that first time, but every single week. Week after week, for the rest of their lives, widowed women were subjected to the humiliation of a man scraping their scalp with a straight razor, all so that they would be unattractive to men. Baya, after she decided that she would marry Annah, finally let her hair grow out. She writes in her autobiography that on the 11th of March, 1889, when the Sharada Sadan School opened in Bombay, she, at the age of twenty-four, four years past the maximum admission age, was the first student enrolled in the school. This was where she lived when she and Annah Karve had their first meeting.

Although they were married under British civil law, in the eyes of all Pune this was not a couple, but a sinful cohabitation. Hindu morality was outraged and incensed. Annah and his widow-wife Baya were ostracised from society. On the newly married couple's visit to Annah's mother and brother in Murud in Konkan, they had to live in the cowshed. If they had stayed in the house, the village would have excommunicated the family. In Pune, besides being humiliated and insulted and even spat upon, no one would rent them a place to live. They were forced to live outside the city limits, on a haunted heath, in huts that they and others like themselves built. When Baya was pregnant and close to her time, she walked to the hospital—miles and miles—to spend the night there in case she went into labour. When the child did not come in the night, she walked back home in the morning to take care of all the widows and orphans and other unfortunates that lived out there with them.

By the time Irawati met Annah Karve, this assemblage of huts out in the dusty distance of the city had become an orphanage and the first women's university in the country. Irawati, though she had become accustomed to living in a house where education was valued, had not forgotten how she had to fight and argue with her own father for each and every year of her own education. She had not forgotten her father's declaration, 'Once your marriage is done, my responsibility is done.'

Annah Karve impressed her. She knew that what he thought and believed, and what he had done for widows and women, was not ordinary. He had endured so much hatred and ridicule, as had his wife, as had their children, to do what he did, when he could have lived the privileged life of a professor of mathematics, and a Chitpavan Brahmin in Pune or Bombay.

Appa Paranjpye, and his cousin Annah Karve, were among the prominent personalities of Pune. But unlike Appa, Annah and his sons were among those considered eccentric, and even unwanted in society. They were ostracised from most polite society. They were, however, family, and always welcome in the Paranjpye house, and they were often visitors there.

~

Pune beyond the Mutha river was mostly uninhabited when Irawati crossed it for the first time. A group of Punekars, some of whom had recently become wealthy and some who had high positions in the British government, had bought the vacant land, built houses for themselves, and established a residential colony there. It was there that Ganesh Karmarkar bought a plot and built a bungalow when he returned to Pune from Myingyan. He was one of the nouveau riche, and he settled down among the other residents of the colony who included rich men like himself, others who were highly educated, civil servants and reformists. Irawati then returned to live with her own family. Any awkwardness or difficulty adapting to a family that was her own but unfamiliar was eased by the proximity to Shakuntala, Saitai, and Appa. They were a short walk away, and a comfort to her as she reacquainted herself with her brothers and parents, and they with her. This colony was modelled after British Cantonment towns. In the centre of the residential area was a clubhouse with billiards and table tennis, and tennis courts. It was here that Irawati and Shakuntala, Irawati's brothers, as well as Annah Karve's sons, all spent their leisure time. They played tennis and learned to swim. The abandoned and disused stone quarry on the land became an enormous swimming 'tank'—it had a length of over a hundred metres. Being just a hole in the ground, there was no smooth floor, and there were corners of it that were murky, the stone walls slippery with moss. Irawati became a lifelong swimmer. Unlike the other ladies who would lift their sarees up to their ankles and step gingerly into bodies of water, Irawati would don her bathing suit and navigate pools, lakes, and rivers with her fine confident breaststroke.

Even during the time Irawati was in Bombay with Appa and Shakuntala and Saitai, doing her Master's degree, there were visits home to Pune. It was inevitable that she would come into contact with the brothers Shankar, Dinkar and Bhaskar Karve.

Raghunath, Annah Karve's oldest son and only child from Annah's first marriage, was also well known to Irawati, as he was close to Appa Paranjpye and Saitai, and also Shakuntala. This Karve was a social outcast for another reason. On top of his father's unacceptable and sinful deeds, Raghunath, or 'Radhon' as he was known, was a pioneer in family planning and sexual health. There was no end to shaking of heads and clucking of tongues—this man was talking publicly about birth control for all. This was more than enough to lose him his job as a professor of mathematics at Wilson College in Bombay: he was advocating for something that his Christian masters could not possibly abide and condone. Not to stop there, he began to talk about something so taboo that it would be half a century before it became an acceptable topic of discussion: women's right to sex—and sexual pleasure. He had his supporters, and some who fondly said his thinking was the result of his being educated in France, because, of course, peculiar ideas about sexuality must come from France. When he found that no respectable publication would consider broadcasting his thoughts, he started his own paper called *Samajswasthya*—society's health—which was also derided and frowned upon as lewd and even pornographic. All this would have put him far beyond the pale of any society, let alone in 1920s India.[13]

~

Ganesh Karmarkar had been plotting his daughter's marriage for some time. He had tried and tried to get her to end her education every year. Every year he could see his Irawati becoming less marriageable, and more strange, perhaps more and more a Paranjpye, and less a Karmarkar. It would not be hard to imagine that he might have regretted his decision, if at all it was in his hands, to allow his only daughter to be brought up by this family, and in particular R.P. Paranjpye—a liberal, an atheist, a man unconventional in ways that could only have been unacceptable to Irawati's father, also because R.P. Paranjpye was a man who encouraged women toward higher education, and one who clearly did not share the same ideas as himself about Irawati herself.

As she worked toward her Master's degree in sociology, she began to wonder how she would continue her path of study, how she would move toward more knowledge, forever. It must have been a strange time in her life, caught between her father, who wanted a life for her that had nothing to do with who she had become under the benevolent gaze of her other father, and her own deep desire to continue to be who she had become. Irawati was aware of her own mind, her place in the world, she had a sense of the possibility of her future. She could not possibly have accepted life as wife to a minor princeling however much luxury and security this life promised. Whether it was an actual plot then, between her, and Shakuntala, and Saitai and Appa Paranjpye, or whether things fell into place without words and agreements, she went to her father with a counterproposal: she would marry, but it would be someone of her own choice. It would in fact be Dinkar Karve, second of the four sons of Dhondo Keshav Karve. Apart from being a mild-mannered, gentle, and reasonably handsome young man, this was the son of the man who believed and worked for the education of women, who had started the first university for women in the country—surely this was the easy way to ensure her own academic future. Besides, the Karves were part of the larger Paranjpye family, so she knew that Appa, at least, would surely approve of the match.

Ganesh Karmarkar, however, was another matter. There was an earthquake. He refused to even consider such a preposterous prospect. Marrying the Frog Prince would have brought less disapproval and dismay from Irawati's father. Her mother, and her brothers, who knew Dinkar Karve and his family, perhaps did not feel as badly about their Irawati becoming a Karve. Bhagirathi, Irawati's mother, was after all an educated woman herself. She must have understood to some extent what her daughter wanted—and perhaps even wished that Irawati could live a life that she, Bhagirathi, had not. But apart from this, she herself had met the young man, and was fond of him. He had visited the Karmarkar household, he was friends with her sons, he had even eaten meals at their house. She had warmed to his appreciation for her cooking (which she did without any onions or garlic), which may or may not have been because his own mother, Baya, was a terrible cook.

Bhagirathi then, openly took her daughter's side, and so did all the five brothers, and then, Appa Paranjpye spoke to the already isolated Ganesh Karmarkar. This was the last straw, but it did not yet break the camel's back. In fact, when R.P. talked to him about the deep idealism and integrity of the Karves, and recounted to him the enormous sacrifices the members of this family had made in their personal, and professional lives in order to do the work of improving and progressing some of the terrible social practices of the state and the country, it made matters even worse for Ganesh Karmarkar.

The story he had heard was that, well educated though they all were, the Karve boys had paid for this education with a loan from a grain merchant. This was true. Baya and Annah Karve really did not have any money, commensurate with the unfortunate reality of any social worker's life anywhere in the world. Their son Shankar wished to go to England to study medicine. It was Baya who was always the doer, and her reputation of being a bit of a dragon probably helped her. She went to the grain merchant from whom she bought supplies for the hostel, and she asked him for a loan. She gave him her word that it would be repaid. She didn't tell him when, and, possibly intimidated by the unseen scales and fire, he did not ask. He took her word, and he gave her the money. Shankar went to England, got his medical degree, and moved to South Africa to practise medicine there. Baya, before making Shankar repay the grain merchant, made him pay for the education of his younger brother. The grain merchant did get his money back—when all the Karve sons were educated, including Dinkar, who got his PhD in chemistry, in the German city of Leipzig.

For Ganesh Karmarkar, all this made them nothing more than poverty stricken social workers. How were they going to be able to look after his daughter? All that their idealism and integrity and social improvement projects had got them was being fired from paying jobs, having to live out in the perimeter of the city both socially and literally, beg from individuals and companies for money for their own and their institutions' expenses because social work was seen as charity and not the task of the state, and earn the disapproval of the society that he was a part of. But it was the Karve family's financial situation that worried him the most. He had harboured dreams of a royal wedding and a sumptuous married life for his daughter, and he could not imagine what sort of life she would have in this poor and famously peculiar family. He could not allow it.

Ganesh Karmarkar was quite alone in his dissent, if he didn't count the support of all of Pune society. In his own family, even the fact that he was the patriarch could not overcome what seemed like a foregone conclusion.

Irawati Karmarkar and Dinkar Karve were married in Pune in 1926. Given that the Karve-Paranjpye contingent consisted of a phalanx of militant atheists, the marriage itself was simple. Also, all was not hearts and flowers. Irawati reports being angry and upset about the behaviour and lack of understanding of unspecified people. The following day the Karves hosted a big dinner for the two families. As is the custom, people took turns to recite poems appropriate for the occasion. As was also the custom, the patriarch of the family, Annah Karve, recited the final verses.

The dearest friend, the entire kinship,
All desires, great treasure, life itself,
To the woman the husband, to the man the wife,
Let this be understood by the young couple.

Irawati says about this moment, 'How clear were his words, like some carving on stone; and as each nectar-filled line fell on my ears, it was engraved on my heart. I became quiet and peaceful and entered into the Karve family with this great blessing.'[14]

~

For a couple who had married in spite of the opposition of one parent, and perhaps the indifference of other family members, their first months of married life were difficult. They were poor, as Ganesh Karmarkar had feared they would be, but Dinkar had a good job as professor of chemistry at the Fergusson College. There was also the fact that Appa Paranjpye, who not only did not oppose the marriage but actively encouraged it, thrilled that his ward had married into his own family, gave the couple a gift of money. Irawati said that, because of their financial situation at that time, that 1,000-rupee gift was equal to 10,000 to them. By today's standards it may have been a paltry sum, but in 1926, it meant that they did not have to worry too much about their immediate future.

Dinkar Karve has been heard, over all the decades of his marriage to Irawati and quoted by many, as saying how clever she was, how brilliant. He would say matter-of-factly, as he said most things, and quite unselfconsciously, that he always knew, from the time he first met her, that she was more intelligent than himself. He was in no doubt that she, if she so desired, must continue her education.

Irawati had completed her Master's degree at the University of Bombay, where a sociology department had opened less than a decade before. Her thesis studied cultural, social, and physical characteristics of her own caste community, the Chitpavan Brahmins of Western Maharashtra. Her MA thesis supervisor, Professor G.S. Ghurye, would perhaps have been a less absent supervisor if he had not been busy doing the pioneering work of heading the nascent department and writing articles and books on Indian society: this was a time when India was yet to be studied by sociologists and anthropologists, who were a very small professional group in the country. Although the subcontinent was such an interesting site for research, science resources were meagre, and doing a PhD in anthropology in India was simply not an option. It hadn't been an option for Ghurye, who had gone to the University of Cambridge, or for most Indian anthropologists of that time.

Dinkar, with his own experiences in Germany, felt that Irawati should go there as well to continue her academic career. Of course, neither of them had the funds needed for her education, let alone transport there and back or rent and food and living expenses. But Dinkar was perfectly sure he would find the money, and he knew that Irawati would, once she was there in person, be able to get funding from scholarships from the universities and the German government. Before everything else, though, he went to the one person they knew would be behind them in this enterprise, the person who believed all women should get an education—his father, Annah Karve. After all, he enthusiastically sponsored women from his institutions quite regularly to go abroad for higher studies. The young, recently married couple felt they must get his blessings, and they were quite confident that they would. But what they heard from him was:

'Doctoral studies? Germany? Whatever for? She can get a job in the Women's University without any further degree. And the expense? I am against this. I am not in favour of this plan at all.'

Dinu was shocked and confused, and Irawati was bitter about it. When women who were graduates or employees of his own institutions, even those who were not particularly good at their studies, were encouraged and supported by Annah, why was she, his own daughter-in-law, who clearly shone in hers, treated this way? She did get over her bitterness, eventually, when the passage of decades had given her an understanding of the man and dissolved her anger. But when she packed her bags for Germany and set off on that long and lonely journey, it was without the blessings of the great personage who was her father-in-law, Annah Karve, and she felt this privation keenly. The other women of the Karve family, but by no means only the women, including her mother-in-law, disliked Irawati and what they perceived as her unfair privilege. They felt resentful toward her, because she got to go away and study—something they clearly saw as a luxury, and easier to do than what they had to do, which was stay home and do housework.

Irawati did not have the support then, of either the Karmarkars or the Karves. What she did have was Dinu's support, and his confidence and belief in her. These she took with her into the unknown world that awaited her, over the sea, in the city of Berlin.

Part Three

8

Grihasti Parva

In *Yuganta*, Irawati's essays on her precious Mahabharata, she ends her chapter on its main female protagonist Draupadi with what she self-deprecatingly calls her naroti—a coconut shell—meaning a worthless thing. But this contemplation of Draupadi's thoughts as she lay on a cold Himalayan slope in the last moments of that life is intense and tragic and beautiful. Draupadi is a woman, a princess, who has been shared by five husbands, who suffered immeasurably because of these five men's stupidity, arrogance, greed, weaknesses. And here, in her dying moments, in Irawati's interpretation, Draupadi thinks about those husbands: Arjun, the one who won her, whom she loved most, the finest archer in the land, whose heart belonged to Krishna. Dharma, the eldest, who knew, though she tried to love them all equally, who it was that she loved above all. And then realisation comes to her in images: it was Bhima, the brutish, the unsophisticated, the biggest of the five, who loved her more than any of her other husbands did.

> *Bhima ready to burn the hands of his older brother who lost her, Draupadi, in a game of dice, Bhima so angry that he had to be held down by Arjuna, Bhima*

> *comforting her when she was tired, Bhima bringing her fragrant lotuses, Bhima drinking the blood of the man who had insulted her, Bhima plaiting her hair with his bloody hands, Bhima who killed her enemies, Bhima who loved her.*[15]

Irawati's Draupadi's last words are to Bhima:

> *In our next birth, be the eldest, Bhima. Under your shelter we can live in safety and joy.*[16]

According to Irawati, many self-serving interpolations and deletions have influenced the meanings and the intent of the original story in the Mahabharata, particularly after the Jain Puranas. If her own piece were to be added to it, it would only enhance the epic. Whatever she says, it is not an empty coconut shell. Perhaps, in her portrayal of this great love of Bhima's for Draupadi lies her acknowledgment of someone in her own life. The wives and partners of great or accomplished men are rarely given the credit and accolades or even acknowledgement they deserve. Their support to their husbands and partners and sons is simply assumed. When it is a woman who has achieved much or is famous, however, their husbands are praised greatly, even credited for her accomplishments. Irawati herself chafed against such treatment, and was bitter about repeatedly being recognised only in relation to the men in her life. Feminists, of whatever gender, should no doubt expect the support of their partners, of whatever gender. But in the time and place that Irawati and her husband Dinu lived their lives, it would be remiss not to acknowledge, and give credit, to Irawati's husband. In her case, although Dinu was no brute—nor was he earthy, tempestuous or rough like Bhima—he was the one who quietly smoothed her path in life. If these things are remarkable, they are more so because this is a middle-class Indian man in 1920s Pune. It was after all more likely that he would have been more like Ram of the Ramayana, the so-called ideal man of Hindu India (who failed his wife utterly at the end), and less like Bhima. But that was not the case.

Irawati, in her husband Dinu, had a champion, a partner, a lover, an admirer, a friend, and a companion in every way. He was a fellow academic who would read and discuss and even carefully edit her writing, both in English and Marathi. He travelled with her when he could, to see the country and the world, often putting her needs before his own. If in fact it is true that Irawati married him because she saw him as a way to more education, then she got so much more than she could have hoped for. So much more than any woman of her time could have asked for. It might have been that he was influenced by the views and actions of his own father whose support of women was legendary, or his brother who also did works of great importance to women. Whatever be the reason, Dinu had a finely developed sense of justice and fairness. Irawati could be considered among those rare people whose partners understood who they were, what they were capable of, and what support they needed to achieve it. There was nothing more that she could have asked for in a life companion. This soft-spoken, deeply intelligent, handsome man, on top of all these virtues, adored his wife. There was no envy or competition that he felt, or any male ego that came into play in his feelings toward her. He was quite clear that she was a special and unique woman, and it was not that he *permitted*, or *allowed* her to do what she desired—he never thought of it in that way. In spite of the opposition of her father and his own father, he made it possible—in fact, insisted she go to Germany for her doctoral studies, but when she returned, he was there, all through her life, helping her achieve all that she did. It would not be the slightest exaggeration to say that behind this remarkable woman was her remarkable husband.

If someone was determined to find something wanting in Dinu, the obvious was that he was not a wealthy man. This fact had not stood in his way when he needed the money to get something done. He did not feel the false shame that is sometimes thrust upon and borne by people who are poor. Like his father, he went to people who had the means, and asked for the money he needed. For Irawati's Germany stay, he went to an industrialist known to the Karve family—Jeevraj Mehta. Dinu promised to repay the money, which eventually he and Irawati did. But, although Irawati herself never did, her brothers and father felt that Irawati, married as she was to a poor college professor, son of a social worker, must be living in poverty and having to do without the comforts of life that she was used to, or that they felt she should have. One of the brothers worked in construction, and, between them, they built a house for Irawati and Dinu. Situated on the broad side of a long triangular plot of land on Law College Road in Pune, this house was where they lived for most of their lives together. They paid Irawati's brothers back, as Dinu has recorded in his diaries of accounts—among other entries such as groceries and maternity expenses.

The garden of this house was Dinu's pride and joy. He grew fruit trees there, which he started from seedlings and cuttings that he acquired from friends and travels. Mangoes, papayas, guavas, chikoos, jamun, big and small gooseberries, moringa grew there, even a coconut palm, and bananas and colocasia by the kitchen drain. Besides all these fruits and ornamental plants, Dinu also grew herbs and vegetables. They brought back flowering shrubs—plants and seeds from travels all over the country. Irawati would carry or mail seeds back to Pune from her field trips and other travels, friends would bring Dinu cuttings, and he himself collected plants and flowers that he liked from wherever he saw them. There were many varieties of every flower—clematis, gerbera, china rose, bougainvillaea on the perimeter, wisteria, jacaranda, gulmohar, hibiscus. And jasmine. There were seven varieties of jasmine in Dinu's garden, the flowers all subtly different in colour and size and shape, and fragrance too. This was Irawati and Dinu's favourite. It was no surprise then, that their first child, born on October 11, 1932, was named Jai—their jasmine daughter.

Irawati and Dinu had three children—after Jai came Anand in 1935, and then Gauri, the youngest, a little bit later, in 1942. They all grew up in the house on Law College Road. They went to Ahilyabai Holkar school, and then Fergusson College, and they all remember a very happy childhood lived there, with their parents who were both professors. The house was often full of children—the three Karve children, their neighbours and friends, the Gadgil's children, their cousins Chandu and Kamal, and Shakuntala's daughter Sai, as well as many cousins. There were dogs, rabbits, and several cats—who came and went as they pleased.

On one of Irawati's field trips, one evening, the forest ranger came over to the bungalow where she was staying with Anand, Chandu and Kamal. The man took something out of his pocket and placed it on the table. To their amazement, they saw it was a tiny, miniature deer.

'I waited and waited for the mother to return,' the ranger said, 'it will die for sure. I thought I would bring it for you to see.'

'What is it?' they asked him.

'Mouse deer,' he said, 'even the adults are small, and this fellow is just a baby.'

Irawati and the children fed it milk through a rubber tube, and it survived. When it was time for them to leave, they took it home with them. The fellow was a female, and they named her Honey after the honey gatherer people of the area she came from, and she, too, lived a long time with them. Gauri remembers Dinu looking after the little animal, along with the other cats and dogs and children.

Occasionally their maternal grandmother, Bhagirathi, whom they called Aai, came to look after them, particularly when Irawati went away on field trips during her semester breaks. Bhagirathi was extremely fond of her son-in-law, Dinu, even before he became her son-in-law. According to Gauri, she tried to teach her younger granddaughter to cook and sew, and many other skills that she thought a girl should have. But Gauri was more interested in climbing the trees and running in the neighbourhood with her friends. Bhagirathi's own daughter Irawati could sew and knit, and crochet, and even do smocking. Gauri too, learned, and taught herself various crafts, but not as a young girl, and certainly not from her grandmother. She did learn to make 'gulkand', which she brilliantly translated into English as 'Rose Jam'—which later became the title of a short story in which she describes her two grandmothers.[17]

According to Gauri, Irawati's mother-in-law, the redoubtable and by then cantankerous Baya, did not often come to stay with them, she had soured relations with most of her relatives. Although she had very much wanted daughters, and even dressed her youngest son—Dinu's younger brother Bhaskar—in girl's clothes till he was old enough to go to school, she did not get along with her own daughters-in-law. She particularly disliked Irawati and her education and independence, and made no secret of it. She had grown up extremely poor and had had an extremely hard life. To her, Irawati's habits seemed overindulgent and decadent. When Baya did come to the house to visit, she would mumble and mutter endlessly about it all, the profligacy and waste and how she would never do this or that thing that her daughter-in-law did. One day, Gauri recalls, Irawati was holding a large pot of freshly pasteurised milk. Hearing the usual litany against her, she lost her patience. She held the milk over the kitchen sink and said to her mother-in-law, 'I can do what I want. I have a job, I earn as much as my husband does, I don't need anyone to tell me what to do with it. See this milk? I can pour this all down the sink if I want to.' That might have been a turning point in their relationship.

When Annah Karve was too old and frail to live on his own, and when his wife Baya was too old and infirm to look after him, he moved in with Irawati and Dinu. Given the state of affairs between Baya and her sons' wives, it seemed prudent that Baya did not go to live with any of them. Instead, she went to live in Hingne at the Hindu Widows' Home that her husband had founded. There she was quite content, lording it over all the women, the residents as well as administrators and matrons.

Irawati's relationship with her father-in-law, Dhondo Keshav Karve, a now well-established legend and patriarch of Maharashtra, had not begun in the best way. He had, after all, opposed her further education in Germany, and even suggested that she could get a job without more education. Even so, he was her father-in-law, and live with them he did. Irawati was nothing if not an observer of people. Annah

Karve was interesting to her, with his peculiarly stoic attitude toward his family and loved ones, but his highly emotional relationship with his institutions. In her essay about him (translated by Dinu as 'Grandfather'[18]) she recalls when Annah was in his late nineties and his son passed away. Irawati was in an adjoining room working, and could hear the conversations between Annah and visitors who had come to commiserate with him after the funeral. People were expressing their deepest sympathies, telling him how sorry they were for his loss. Everyone saw it as a terrible loss, as did she. The loss of a child, however old the parent, was, after all, a tragedy and not the natural order of things. So when Irawati heard what Annah said to his visitors, it shocked her to the core, and stayed with her.

'Well, everyone has to die, and he was old and infirm.'

Irawati was unnerved by Annah. Being herself an emotional and passionate person, she struggled to understand his attitudes, his indifference and subsequent, even if unintentional, cruelty to the people closest to him. She did eventually come to a conclusion, after puzzling about him and observing him for decades: that he was what is known as sthitapradnya—a wise one.

One Diwali the family had all gone to Hyderabad to visit Irawati's brother there. She was not one to rise early on holidays, but her brother and Annah did, and after his tea, Annah took a walk in the garden. His words on the auspicious first day of the Hindu year were an inspiration to her: 'Do not allow the lamp of knowledge in your heart be extinguished,' he said, in his sweet and pleasant voice.

Although it ends on a reconciliatory and even fond note, Irawati's essay 'Grandfather' is not entirely flattering to the venerable old man of Maharashtra. She talks about how he seemed almost uncaring to his wife and children, how he was almost childlike in some ways, and how, though he did not seek them out, he did not eschew the pleasures of life. Irawati wrote that Annah Karve liked good food when he was given it, enjoyed the performing arts, and appreciated beauty. This could have been seen to be an undesirable trait in one of India's 'great men', particularly as the others of his time, like Gandhi, publicly led lives of austerity, claiming that study should be enough pleasure. Some people were even disappointed when they found out that he drank tea and coffee many times a day! Even so, Dinu not only translated the essay, he included it in his internationally published anthology *The New Brahmans.*[19] It is not every man, let alone an Indian man, who would allow such public outspokenness about the patriarch of a family, but it is likely that it did not occur to Dinu to do otherwise.

~

Jai and Anand were older and less trouble than Gauri, who grew up a little wilder than her siblings, and, like all youngest children, had a little more freedom than her older brother and sister. By the time the third, and in this case late, and perhaps, a surprise child comes along, many parents have gotten over the seriousness of childrearing and discipline, have loosened their reins or dispensed with them altogether. Many a time, it is also the case that parents are at a point in their careers that makes greater demands on their time and energy, something they have less of as they are also older than they were during the early years of their children's lives. Two college professors do not make a lot of money, and Irawati and Dinu did not buy things or toys for the children, they never had enough spare money for that. But they never wanted for anything. Cricket bats were any good stick, and a ball was wadded up mud and straw held together by Irawati's crochet. Gauri also recalls her parents taking on piles and piles of exam papers to correct during holidays to make a bit extra. Dinu's vegetable garden saved them grocery money, and his sewing expertise kept clothes going much longer than the children liked, particularly Gauri, who got them last.

Gauri, when speaking of Dinu, says that it was perhaps the equal division of labour in their family that ruined her for other men. Dinu looked after the house and children, including dressing and grooming them when they were not old enough to do so themselves, when Irawati was away, with the help of his mother-in-law when she was available. He did things that were unusual for a man to do, except that the children, particularly Gauri, didn't know it until she went out in the world and discovered that other men were not like Dinu. He and Irawati were equally adept at sewing a rip, or embroidering a tablecloth. And they both earned about the same incomes. Neither of her parents had a greater say in just about any aspect of their domestic lives, nor were they anything but equals in the academic and intellectual realm. And then there were the differences in their household from those of their friends. Gauri doubted if her mother ever bought vegetables in the market. Dinu called his wife by her abbreviated first name—Iru—which was not unusual, but no other woman in their acquaintance ever called her husband by his first name. When she was younger, Gauri thought that her friends' fathers had peculiar names such as 'Tay' (Respectful Him) and 'Aho' (Respectfully You, or Thou). Irawati called her husband Dinu. Not only that, but, much to the consternation of the people who knew them, the children called their parents by the same names they called each other: Iru and Dinu.

Their family life was undergirded with a sort of intellectual enthusiasm. Relatives and neighbours gathered for card games in the hot Pune afternoons, or they did jigsaw puzzles; they played word games and geography games; they made lanterns if there was a festival like Diwali, and they read. Everyone read and read and read. Irawati and Dinu would fight over the crossword in the daily paper until, in their later years of relative prosperity, they decided to splurge and get two subscriptions, so that they could each have their own copy of the crossword.

The Karve children were very much a part of the Paranjpye household as well. They called the Wrangler Appa-Ajoba. Appa's own granddaughter, Shakuntala's daughter Sai, was closest in age, and closest to, Gauri. Gauri, like her mother, adored her third grandfather. To Appa Paranjpye, Sai and Gauri were the next generation, another, different set of Bennet girls. He called them Kitty and Lydia after the two younger, sillier Bennet sisters from *Pride and Prejudice*, the ones who giggled and swooned about the men in regimental uniforms at the nearby military encampment. Silly or not, they too learned their classics under the vigilant eye and ear of Appa Paranjpye, and Gauri went on to do a PhD in English literature, which she attributed at least partly to the influence of the same man who was so important to her mother. It was said of the Karve children, 'Nandu and Jai are Karves. Gauri is a Paranjpye.'

Irawati was brought up in the atheist Paranjpye household, and married into an atheist family. Dinu was always very clear about his thinking. He did not harbour any doubts about gods or about religions, he had no beliefs not based in reason, if in fact he had any beliefs at all. However, he did not ever look down on or demean anyone else's beliefs or need to practise the rituals of their religion. Later in his life, Dinu was annoyed by the muezzin, particularly when they strung up loudspeakers to the walls of the mosque and blasted him out of his sleep or work, and he complained about Diwali firecrackers and the five times a day aartis sung for Ganpati on large music systems set up at every corner, and the traffic jams on immersion day. But when the children were younger, he made no objections when Ganpati came home and Irawati and the children did aarti. Sweets and special meals were cooked during the time, and then Ganpati was immersed in the garden tank at the end of the festival. On Diwali the children made an adobe fort with Shivaji and his mawlas. They would start this project a few days before Diwali, so that the mustard seeds they sprinkled on the earth around the fort sprouted and made a lush green setting for it. They made cottonwool wicks for the terracotta lamps and lined the windowsills with them. They made the Diwali star that would hang outside the house. Irawati brought up her children with all the rituals of Hindu festivals, at the same time eschewing the symbols of Hindu wifehood herself. She said that all these were cultural aspects of the society they lived in. Dinu accepted this explanation, or in any case, did not object to these and other Hindu observances in their household.

In her own life, Irawati could be seen to be progressive, forward-thinking, feminist even. Still, although she herself eschewed the trappings and signifiers of being a married woman, she was one. She lived, in most ways, a traditional Hindu life, though with its notable exceptions. Jai, her older daughter, married an unusual man: Bon Nimbkar, son of a wealthy industrialist father and a mother who was a

Pennsylvania Quaker, was educated in the United States. He had returned to India to become a farmer. Unusual though this was, the marriage itself was arranged. Though Irawati and Dinu did not exactly oppose the marriage of their son Anand to Gudrun, his German sweetheart, they were not exactly happy or even comfortable with the cultural differences and their impact on the marriage. Those two young people had fallen deeply in love with one another. They clearly did not care about the differences in their culture, their ways, their language, or anything at all. Dinu wrote to Professor Verschuer, who had been one of Irawati's professors in Berlin. He lived in Münster, where the parents of the young woman lived. Verschuer arranged a meeting with all concerned, and Anand and Gudrun had convinced the adults that they would find a way around any eventuality. Irawati and Dinu, so far away and so busy with their own lives, accepted, at last. Love is blind, at least at the outset, and perhaps more solid things, like an intellectual common ground, companionship, and friendship, would undergird the rest of Anand and Gudrun's lives, wherever they chose to be. But, the couple were eventually divorced, and then Irawati arranged Anand's second marriage with a more suitable bride, from a culturally similar background. This might not sound so alien in a country where most people marry within their caste group, but the Karve couple and their descendants actually did not care much about caste endogamy, or even religious endogamy: however, a German wife was more than they were willing to happily bless—perhaps because they personally knew Germans and their oddness too well.

Gauri's rebelliousness and sexuality was a strain on her mother's heart, and her marriage too, was arranged, to the first young man she claimed to be serious about—when she was nineteen years old. She also said, privately and in public interviews, that her mother did not approve, nor did she support Gauri when, inevitably, she left that marriage. In fact, Gauri was told that there was no real reason for her to leave the husband, who was an ideal man after all, because he did not beat her or womanise or drink—a standard so low that Gauri sees her mother as a traditionalist, not a feminist at all. According to Gauri, although Irawati was nothing short of brilliant, Irawati's writing and anthropological work was 'part of her own evolution, not connected to the problems of women'[20]—a harsh comment, certainly, because it dismisses Irawati's crucial intellectual engagement with problems concerning women. But Gauri's remark shows how the perceptions on women's issues continue to change over generations, the younger generations always pushing toward new frontiers. Gauri of course, though she spoke from her position as an icon of Marathi feminist literature, knew the undeniable influence of her mother.

9

Paripurti

Whatever her rebellious younger daughter's view of her mother, and whatever Irawati's ways within her own personal life, it is evident that Irawati's work paid constant attention to women in every strata of society, in their small and large struggles, in real life and in the epics. Indeed, Irawati inaugurated a now long-standing tradition in Indian scholarship in re-reading epics according to specific critical lenses, establishing the link between the epics and present-day issues. In her analyses of the Ramayana and the Mahabharata, she shed light on the women's lives particularly. Two women, Sita and Draupadi, are the heroines of these two epics. They are both princesses of powerful houses, married into powerful houses. But there, as Irawati points out, the similarity ends. Whereas Sita is a figure of romantic poetry and her life, even in exile, is the stuff of romantic dreams, Draupadi's was one of suffering. Draupadi's husbands did not do honourably by her, but ultimately their fates were entwined in very real ways, and they lived, and died, together. Sita, the ideal woman of India, is the wife of Ram, in the epic poem named for him, the ideal man of the Hindu pantheon. But even as a child and young woman Irawati harboured misgivings, and an intense anger about Ram. She always preferred the wild and angry Shiva of the mountains, and found Ram's behaviour toward Sita unforgivable. The ideal Ram did not defend Sita unconditionally from the public accusation of transgression, and forced her to take a test of purity. This ends in her self-destruction, leaving a blot on the character of this ideal man, who, instead of giving up his kingdom, sacrificed his wife. These events have many interpretations. But what is interesting here to note is that, in a country where women suffer and are unsafe throughout their lives, the chosen hero, the ideal for men to aspire to, is Ram. When Irawati was older, and she heard women sing songs in praise of Ram at various women's institutions (possibly widows' homes and women's shelters) her anger had become tinged with a bitter cynicism—'men like Ram are the reason that such institutions are full, and as such, being the patron, of course his praises should be sung at such places,' she thought.

An old European folk song led her to think about the story of Sita and Ram in yet another way. In the song, a woman who gave birth to eleven children all at once, was murdered by the villagers. They killed the woman because she was an adulterer, and killed all of those eleven children too. There was gossip and rumour about Sita being an adulterer. But then, she gave birth to twin boys. At the time, giving birth to two or more children at the same time was considered absolute proof of unfaithfulness. It was not superstition, it was fact: it was the 'science' of the time. That Irawati made this peculiar connection is not surprising, all her obsessions come together in this thought process: ancient Indian texts, folk songs, the position of women, the patriarchy, and Hinduism.

Irawati wondered how this 'proven adulterer', Sita, is considered the 'Sati-Savitri'—ideal and pure wife and woman.

She concludes that Sita realised she could never live her life with her head held high. She therefore gave up her love, her children and her kingdom in an instant, and chose instead to be immolated and swallowed up by Mother Earth (Sita's actual mother)—and in so doing, she proved the science, and the superstitions, and the whole kingdom wrong. ('If I am pure then take me into your embrace, mother,' she says.)

~

Another remarkable example of Irawati's concern about the lives of women is in her essay *Women and Culture*[21] which examines an aspect of marital relationships. On one of her research trips, Irawati observes a young married couple who are labourers, both living in a small hut near her hosts' house. To her they seem healthy and clearly quite happy with life and each other. She comments that they are a lovely couple, to which her host's wife retorts that the man beats his wife at least once a fortnight. Irawati replies that in that case the beatings seem not to have affected the young woman much. The old gentleman who is her host is upset by her response.

He says, 'What you are saying is quite backward and conservative. 'She isn't affected.' As if this is normal between husbands and wives.'

As he was to accompany Irawati on her travels through the region, Irawati tells him that he should ask every man they will come across if he beats his wife. At the end of a weeks-long trip, not a single man replied with a 'no'. Irawati did not, obviously, think that wife-beating was a good thing. She was simply pointing out that it was an ingrained part of Indian society. Not only was it widespread, it was accepted, and to such an extent that a man who did not beat his wife was the exception, and that this created its own problems: such men were not respected, not only by other men, but in examples she has recounted, even by their wives. Although her view could be seen as anti-women, Irawati had a very nuanced way of looking at the society in which she lived. Adding nuance to complicated and urgent problems was her, as well as many anthropologists', way of contributing to their solution.

Irawati's anthropological gaze did not spare even her own family. Pointing out that this practice of beating wives cuts through every part of Indian society, her essay 'The Ways of Love'[22] describes a conversation between her own mother and father in an excruciatingly personal story. In this conversation, Ganesh says to Bhagirathi that although he does not take her out to the cinema or go on evening walks with her like her sons do with their wives, he loves his wife more because, unlike his sons who all beat their wives, he has never raised his hand on her. The implication is that he loses his respect as a man, and still does what he thinks is right by his wife.

As for her own life, although Irawati was aware of her status, she was nevertheless incensed by how much she had to compromise, and by her treatment as a woman. Apart from her memories of having been dismissed by (all male) professors in her student days, she also talks about another aspect of being an accomplished woman. She vents her feelings in her famous essay 'Paripurti'[23] (fulfillment, completeness), in which she recounts how, even when being presented with a national award, she is introduced as 'wife of' and 'daughter-in-law' of. Indeed, she says, as she was walking home and the neighbourhood boys pointed at her and said 'there goes Nandu's mother,' her introduction was complete. To Irawati's utter frustration, when this essay was published, her sarcasm was misunderstood, and the whole piece was read as a glorification of motherhood and wifehood, adding insult to injury, as it were. The fact that this essay is still, today, being interpreted in these patriarchal terms is very telling: it shows how Irawati's pro-women interventions, written more than fifty years ago, were very progressive at that time and indeed are still current—and necessary—today.

Irawati was always irked by the call for equality of women. 'Why equality? Why do we want equality with men and not something more?' she would ask, when her feminist students or daughters talked about it. While it is entirely possible that Irawati would have married Dinu even if she had not needed to find a way to secure her freedom to continue her education, perhaps she wanted to be free to make her own decisions, to do what she wanted to do, without that attachment to a male human being—to study as much as she wanted, to marry whomever she wanted, or not. Perhaps she is right about that question. Perhaps it was really not equality that she craved, but autonomy.

Not afraid to participate in political debates, Irawati also made her best efforts to influence governmental politics toward women. This is most evident in her policy-oriented *The Indian Woman in 1975*,[24] a pioneering sociological diagnosis and trend assessment on the employment and education of women in India, and one of the first studies of its kind in India. Written a decade before the year contained in its title, the article analyses an array of quantitative data on women's quality of life and makes some suggestions for policymaking concerning the uplifting of women. Irawati opens the article by talking about a dimension of gender inequality that is, sadly, still true today, and not just in India: girls suffer more than boys, she says, but more than that, at most ages, the vulnerability of female lives is greater than that of males.

She points out the somewhat startling fact that the sex ratio, which she calls the 'deteriorating sex ratio'—because it was changing toward there being more men than women at that time—is better in 'tribal' areas, and worsens with urbanisation and industrialization. The 'deteriorating sex ratio' is a direct effect of the higher vulnerability and mortality of women and girls, which, perhaps surprisingly for most urbanites, was not as aggravated in Adivasi communities, where, as some anthropologists will know, women might enjoy more freedom and more gender equity. In a nutshell, Irawati's *The Indian Woman in 1975* shows that women are the underprivileged in Indian, and other societies, because they are poorer, more vulnerable, and also simply *because* they are women. In other words, the assigned social marker 'female' will determine several social disadvantages to a woman, from childhood to adulthood. Two song couplets collected in Irawati's *Kinship Organisation in India*[25] illustrate some sentiments born with this marker:

> *By some mistake God gave me the birth of a woman. Like a hired bullock which is hard driven by all, I am on the point of breaking.*
>
> *God Rama, I fall to your feet and fold my hands and pray to you, never again give me the birth of a woman.*[26]

In this gender inequality forecast for 1975, Irawati praises the founders of the Indian Constitution for their recognition that ignorance and backwardness were a threat to democracy, and for making education free and compulsory for all children up to the age of fourteen. By making education one of the Directive Principles of the Constitution, she says, '…the biggest democracy in the world committed to the ideals of socialism.'[27] Her desire for her country to pursue this socialism-leaning path is also visible in the pro-labour solutions she finds for problems she encountered. For example, one of the issues in the employment of women in industrial and factory settings was that women could not do the third shift, and needed more rest periods, and therefore factory employers preferred to hire men. Irawati's solution for this discrimination against women was a universal one, of better labour rights for all: 'Compulsory rest periods for men and women would eliminate one of the reasons for discrimination against women.'[28]

Finally she states, removing any doubt as to her feelings about the future of Indian society: 'Social justice in essence requires that the distributive mechanism will operate in favour of the underprivileged.'[29]

As for her own labour conditions, Irawati worked all her adult life, immersing herself so deeply into her writing and reading that she sometimes forgot her life outside of her work. Late one afternoon she was at her desk in her office at Deccan College. While a pile of students' essays waited to be graded, several books lay open beside her, and she was lost in writing. At some point she remembered someone had brought a cup of tea in for her and she took a sip of it. It was cold. She didn't really notice and kept working. She was distracted by a sudden shiver going through her, and realised that her sari and blouse were wet through. She thought that she must have spilled some of the tea on herself. And then she remembered, something which had left her entirely for the past hour. She had a baby girl at home, whose existence she had forgotten, and who must now be very hungry. Nature had its own way of reminding her—she was soaked in breast-milk. She picked up a stack of files and papers and held them to her chest to cover her wet blouse and hurriedly left the office.

~

The much-loved Marathi writer and scholar, Narhar Ambadas Kurundkar, who revered Irawati and also was a critic of her work, considered himself like a son to her. He wrote in the careful and loving work he calls 'A Tribute'[30] published at the end of Irawati's book *Sanskruti*[31] that Irawati embodied, in a single person, a scholar, a homemaker, and a poet. He forgot to add, she was an astute and sensitive observer of people, not excluding herself. But perhaps, that is a part of the poet in her.

One day, after teaching a class on the theory of evolution, Irawati went to buy vegetables for dinner that evening, and ran into an old friend at the market. On the way home, she is thinking about how hard this woman's life has been, how giving and long-suffering she is, to the point of working to educate her many siblings, marry off her sisters, even support them all, but never herself marrying or having her own family. Irawati acknowledges that her own life is the opposite: she is the favourite daughter, adored and spoiled in two households, married to a man who is made of compassion, and children play in their courtyard. Even to be able to fret about this friend, she recognises, is a kind of privilege. Comparing herself to this woman, she feels she is the taker, literally getting bigger and bigger, and that woman a giver, who is shrinking, smaller every time Irawati sees her.

This personal interaction connects in her mind to the class she has taught that day, and to the women of India who are selfless, whose sacrifice is never acknowledged, who, when they are home tired from work, are never given a cup of tea or any sympathy as a working man would be. Like worker ants, she says, they run the households of others, pay off the debts of others, suffer for others, and die childless. And because of them, the selfish and demanding are able to pass on their genes.

Irawati's inward gaze, and her desire to imagine and relate to the suffering of others is the foundation of many of her Marathi essays. Sometimes they are so intensely personal that they feel almost confessional. In one, she writes how, after the marriage of Jai, she felt the walls of the house closing in on her. Anand, following his parents' path, was in Germany, and Gauri, bored at home in the summer holidays, had gone off with her sister to Phaltan. Irawati, lying in her favourite room in the house for a siesta, thinks about how quiet it is. She is at first angry that these travellers gather in her house, eat and drink, bring her so much joy, make her laugh, and then they pack up and leave her, and bring her sorrow and tears. And then she is angry with herself, because it was she who had Jai married, and she who encouraged Anand to go to Germany to study.

She feels she is inside a pyramid, entombed, alone.

Her thoughts turn, of course, to other women. She looks at the photographs of her mother and mother-in-law, face to face on the walls on both sides of her. Her mother-in-law, Baya, was always so excited and happy when her son Shankar was to visit from Africa, and Irawati remembered her suffering and tears when he left after his visit. She understood that anguish now. Irawati missed her own children so much that she actually wished all mothers would die when their children were ten years old.

When Dinu came home from work that evening he was concerned about her. Her eyes were red and swollen from weeping. When she told him she missed her children, he consoled her, but in his logical way. She said, trying to be logical too, 'Gauri should have stayed and done some reading rather than idling away the summer.' He reminded his wife of what she had done after her BA exams, in Pune: she played tennis, and she swam and swam, and did not read a single thing.

As they did when she was troubled, Irawati's thoughts turned to Vithoba.[32] How many years she had been going to Pandharpur, to lay her head on the feet of a stone deity. Why do women go to Pandharpur? They make up a large contingent of the annual pilgrimage to the temple. Irawati thought how pleasant the cool stone of Vithoba's feet felt on her forehead. This god, this Krishna, this wanderer who could not be held for too long in any one place, he was held for twenty-eight yugas in Pandharpur. If gods are made from wishes, then this god, surely, was made by the woman in the pyramid: her captive Krishna, her solace.

And then, she acknowledged how she had hurt another woman, her own mother, when she had prayed to be sent far away from her, and knew that even unintended cruelties can never be undone, not in one's lifetime.

10

Saraswati

The Deccan College is the oldest higher educational institution in all of Western India, founded in 1821, with a grant by the British Government. It was called Hindoo College in its early days. The Mutha river—which Irawati would cross years later to begin her life in the Paranjpye household—flowed between the Deccan College campus and, at the time, most of the city's population. There were no convenient bridges as yet, and students had to take small boats to get across, for a price. Naturally, the enrollment dwindled to a point where the British Government, in 1934, closed it down. This was unacceptable to the illustrious alumni[33] of the college who, after questioning the legitimacy of the action in court, eventually settled with the British. The college was reopened in 1939, this time as a research institution, although it retained the word College in its name.

For most of her life after 1939, this institution was Irawati's place of work. Iru and Dinu's house was also on that side of the Mutha river, which was no longer as cut off as in times past. In the 1940s Irawati acquired a motor scooter, and along with it, the fame of being the only woman to ride around the streets of Pune on it. Dinu would go out and check every single morning, before Irawati went to work, that the tyres were not soft, and that there was enough petrol in it, and then he would put a ten-rupee note in her wallet, if he found it low on funds.

On her daily route to Deccan College, Irawati passed the house of one 'Nasi' Phadke. Narayan Sitaram Phadke was a prolific and popular writer. He had separated from his wife of many years and was living with a much younger woman—a scandal at the time. This man made a public comment about Irawati. He said, 'Even Saraswati herself must ride a scooter.' Irawati reacted with irritation and annoyance when she first heard it, and whenever she heard it afterwards, which was often. There is no consensus, however, on the reason for Irawati's annoyance. It might have been, some think, her low opinion of his writing—mushy romances—rather than the age or legal status of Phadke's partner, or his eugenicist views on population control in India, like allowing only the healthiest specimens to breed, and even then, limiting the number of progeny.

Irawati, this Saraswati, the goddess of learning herself, was one of the Three Gods of Deccan College, as they were known. The other two were H.D. Sankalia in the archaeology department and S.M. Katre in the linguistics department. During the college semesters she taught different courses—with topics ranging from sociology to anthropology—and during the holidays she went on field trips to continue her research. On her travels through India to study different people, Irawati also collected many interactions with people she encountered, and impressions of them, which she examined through the wide lens with which she looked at the world—a lens that included history and geography, but also myth and legend, language and ritual, song and poem, oral and written. Her approach to understanding humans, her anthropology, was as holistic as possible. One of the few Indian anthropologists who published widely both in English and vernacular, her way of interpreting and thinking about the world is well known to the Marathi reading public. Her short, but deeply meaningful Marathi essays covered a wide range of subjects.

In 1945-1946, Irawati had been one of the first recipients of the Emslie Horniman Scholarship of the Royal Anthropological Institute of London. The funds had made some of her research and travels possible.[34] But, for a large part of her career, there was no question of being able to pay a student or anyone else to accompany her during fieldwork. As a result, she resorted to family help: Dinu, and both her older children, even nieces and nephews, were recruited as assistants for some of these research trips. This was joyful work to Jai and Anand: both remember these trips with their anthropologist mother in vivid, nostalgic colours.

Preparation for a trip began with the struggle for funding, a struggle that Indian anthropologists today still know very well. Irawati would write research proposals and ask for grants from institutions, foundations and various other sources. Whether she received the money or not, she would use holidays—summer and winter, as well as any religious and bank holidays—to make the trips. Before leaving, she planned as much as she could. She arranged lodgings and transport, and someone to interpret for her if she was going to a part of the country where the language was not one she spoke. Besides Maharashtra, she also went to fieldwork in different corners of the country: in states known today as Karnataka, Odisha, Gujarat and Bihar, to name just a few.

In the summer of 1950, when he was fifteen, Irawati took Anand on his first stint as her assistant. Anand already knew how different his mother was from those of his friends. None of his friends or even anyone in any other family he knew called their parents by their first names, as he and his sisters did. All his friends' mothers wore the symbols that indicated their married status: mangalsutra around their necks, bangles on their arms, and kunku on their foreheads. Iru had none of these. She did have some sort of pendant that she wore, but it could not be called a mangalsutra. It was a small brown stone with a black spot on it, that looked like an eye—Dinu's eye—which was what she called it. No one else's mother was as tall as Iru was, nor taught in a college, nor was invited abroad to give lectures. Nor did any of the mothers drive about town on a motor scooter. Anand knew for certain that no other person his age had a mother who would get into a proper swimsuit (made specially for her in a Pune hosiery factory) and swim a breaststroke from one end of Tilak Tank to the other, a full 100 metres, nonstop. The younger women and girls his age would sometimes get into the water, in their brothers' shorts and shirts, but none of the older ones had conquered the water, like Iru had. And now here was something more that his Iru did that not only no other mother in his acquaintance did, but something that he could actually be part of: anthropological research.

On Anand's first research trip, he accompanied Irawati to the southwestern part of India. They travelled by train and then bus and then finally in a jeep, to a forest bungalow deep in among the trees in a wood within a coffee plantation in the area then known as Coorg, in the Western Ghats in Karnataka. They were there to take blood samples of the Adivasis, Hindi for aboriginal or indigenous people, also called 'tribals' in British colonial parlance. This was done by pricking the finger for a drop of blood, not from a vein with a needle and syringe. Like many other anthropologists of that time, and for the same reason that she measured people's bodies, Irawati studied blood groups frequencies: to try to infer more about the sampled communities and their biological relations to other social groups, based on the theory that different populations would tend to have a different blood group profile.[35] They would collect samples from two Adivasi groups, the Beta Kuruba and the Genu Kuruba—the latter known as a honey collecting tribe—and Irawati planned to compare the samples with non-Adivasi people. For Anand, as a young boy, this was an adventure. The area was not electrified, so they went to bed early after reading for a while by the light of a kerosene lantern. They could hear the hum of insects and occasional calls of owls and nightbirds as they fell asleep. In the morning, very early, after freshening up and eating a meal, they set off in a jeep to a place where local Adivasis would gather, as instructed by the forestry officer.

On the way they passed through a beautiful old teak forest, and Irawati explained to Anand that the officer belonged to the Indian Forestry Service, and his job was to guard the forest they were passing through. During British rule, the forest was seen as a precious resource, and the British even planted teak, quinine, and other trees for future harvests. They established the forestry service, which is much like the police force, and with a similar hierarchy. The forestry service took care of the forests where many Adivasis lived and, the forestry service often being their only intermediary to the state, Adivasis would gather if service officials asked them to do so. Irawati also explained that sickle cell anaemia was, sadly, rampant among them, so they were in a way used to blood samples being drawn, and did not protest or object when she lined them up and took blood, as well as anthropomorphic measurements. Anand wrote down the numbers she called out to him.

When they were done for the day, the jeep driver took them back to the forest bungalow, an almost two-hour drive. In the forest he saw flocks of deer running through the trees, and glimpsed bison too. Though it was already quite dark, their work was not done. They did not have any way to store the blood samples they had taken that day—there was no electricity, let alone any form of refrigeration or ice. They had to do the testing immediately, and record the results for that day. This was Anand's job. He had been Irawati's assistant all day, carrying, writing, washing, following her instructions and doing whatever she needed him to do. Back in the bungalow they readied the items for the sample analysis: a little slab with twelve half-circle indentations in which they would place serum, and then the blood they had collected. These they would mix, and then record which ones coagulated and which did not. When all the samples were tested and the results recorded, Anand washed and dried everything and put it away. They ate a simple dinner prepared for them by the cook—as it would have been for passing civil servants in British times. Then they went to bed, to get enough sleep before another early start.

The next morning they were driven even further away. After waiting a long time they began to worry, there was no sign of any people to collect samples from. The forestry officer was visibly angry, and also surprised, that the men he had asked to come had not arrived. They finally did arrive, all at once, and were quite sanguine, and after talking to them a minute the officer was no longer angry.

'There was a bison delay,' he informed the anthropologist and her assistant. A large herd of gaur bison—the largest wild bovine in the country—moving across their trail had made it impossible for the men to be on time. It was dark before Irawati and Anand made it back to the bungalow after collecting their samples, and late into the night before they finished the analysis to the sounds of the forest in the light of the kerosene lamp.

Anand went on one other trip with his mother, this time to Kerala, where they travelled to Travancore, Malabar, and Cochin. Here they drove hours and back again to remote places to obtain samples from Adivasi communities. They also sampled the Namboodari and Nayyar communities. Anand enjoyed every minute of his trips with his mother. He boasted about it at school, and he never forgot the thrill of seeing wild animals and meeting people who lived in the forests.

~

Jai, too, enjoyed these field trips with her mother, and went on to do her MA in sociology herself. One of the projects Jai did was under her mother's direction. In 1956, Irawati had heard about a dam being built in Western Maharashtra, and about a prehistoric forest nearby. Irawati decided to go there, and she took Jai with her.

The steep walls of the Sahyadri Mountains sloped up from the Koyna River valley. Irawati recognised teak and sal as she walked through the ancient virgin forest, she knew the colours of the birds' wings of the calls she could hear, she knew tigers and leopards hunted spotted deer and bison here. She stopped to look at plants on the forest floor, and up into the great branches and knew that sloth bears slept in them. Her breath shuddered and she rested her back against the broad old bark of a tree so tall, it rose up through the canopy beyond their sight. All the walkers were silent, stunned by the place they had come to see, and bewildered by the sadness that overcame every one of them. Irawati never forgot how she felt in that place which was so old, so powerful, and yet, so vulnerable to the works of men. Within a year from that moment, this valley, these ancient trees, these tigers and sloths and snakes and lizards would all be submerged. Neither she, nor any other person would ever see this place again.

The Koyna Valley, flooded by the lake that formed when the Koyna river was impounded by the building of the dam, like the Khandava forest that had been burned down in the Mahabharata, had its own human inhabitants, and theirs was a different fate from the animals and the forest, and thankfully, from the Naga people of the Khandava forest. They were—whether they wanted it or not—moved before the dam project was completed, and relocated into nearby districts. It was these displaced people that Irawati along with Jai surveyed, in one of the earliest studies of this kind ever done. Forced displacement resulting from development was not common in India—at least not so common as it unfortunately would become later, when the pressure of economic progress became so urgent that communities with little power had virtually no chance to resist when their ancestral lands were in the way of the bulldozer. Irawati and Jai designed and conducted an anthropological field survey that took from July 1965 until January of 1967. Jai did most of the work this time: she met and talked with hundreds of people who had lost their homes and also their lands, their trees, their community and temples, and some their livelihoods. At the same time, not every person was unhappy with their lot, and not every person would have liked to be restored to their past if that was magically possible. This survey gives an intricate and detailed picture of what displacement of this sort looks like, and what worked and what didn't in the Maharashtra government's policies.

Irawati and Jai found out that the younger people were less disturbed than the older ones about their displacement. Irawati writes that people who had literally never handled any form of money who suddenly came into a relatively large sum of compensation did poorly—they often gambled it away or used it for alcohol. The saddest observation, though not surprising in the least, was that the new villages constituted themselves exactly as the old ones had been: the upper and lowest castes were segregated. They also heard eye-witness accounts of those who had not been prepared by the authorities for what was to come—how they had to just take what they could carry and run for their lives, because the water rose so fast, the dam lake swallowing everything on its way as it came into being. The result of their research, *A Survey of the People Displaced Through the Koyna Dam* (1969), was the first such book on the impact of projects of this kind in India, and, a model for future such studies and surveys.[36]

Keeping her eyes open to as many possible aspects of life and humanity an anthropologist can be interested in, Irawati wrote many observations in each of her research trips. In 1959, for example, she went to Assam in the northeast on a government-funded field trip. She travelled extensively in the state collecting data and absorbing every smallest detail, from the passengers at the Calcutta airport going to Guwahati, to the politics of the Adivasis and the effect of Christian missionaries on the hill people. On the drive high up into the Garo Hills, the jeep she was in blew out a tyre, and they missed the window of one-way traffic going up. They left late in the evening when the mountain road opened up again, and Irawati was looking forward to the drive through the lush forests. Maybe, she thought, she would get lucky and would glimpse some animals in the evening light. What she saw was brutal and shocked her to the core. The trees were on fire. Great swathes of the forest were burning, and orange flames lit up the sky. She was stunned and very upset, but also puzzled as to why the driver had no reaction. In Mysore, in Kodagu, she had seen forest officials and rangers react instantly to the slightest wisp of smoke in the precious forests. And here, when everything seemed ablaze and impossible to save, there was no sign of any help coming. The fire was consuming enormous, ancient trees.

'The Garo people burn the forests,' the driver told her, 'they want to plant rice. This is quite normal.'

Irawati stayed that night in a dak bungalow on the very top of a high hill and she could see a field of fire, the glow of hell from up above. The next day, on the drive back down the mountains, the inferno of the night had left a smouldering graveyard of the once magnificent forest, and she did not know which sight was worse. She felt anxiety and despair for what was to come. The Khandava forest in the Mahabharata had been burned down so a city could be built for the Pandava princes. All the trees in the forest perished, and all the animals and birds—in fact every living thing in that precious ecosystem was sacrificed—so that the heroes would have a place to rule. The Mahabharata talks of the snakes that died in the fire. Irawati thinks that these are not snakes, but perhaps forest-dwellers who were murdered in order for the Pandavas to obtain their forest realm. She is quite severely critical of this deed, thought up and brutally carried out mostly by Arjun and Krishna, the revered heroes of the entire Hindu world. She goes so far as to compare them with possibly the best known villain in the history of the world, and one with whom she had a particular historical connection. In her words:

> *In the burning of Khandava no rules of conduct seem to have been observed. The sole aim was the acquisition of land and the liquidation of the Nagas. But the cruel objective was defeated. Just as Hitler found it impossible to wipe out a whole people, so did the Pandavas. All they gained through this cruelty were the curses of hundreds of victims and three generations of enmity.*

Irawati's anger at the immoral destruction of the great Khandava forest, and perhaps a sense that the perpetrators got what they deserved, vibrates in the sentences from the same essay from *Yuganta*, 'The Palace of Maya':

> *The Pandavas lost everything they possessed, and went into exile with nothing but their weapons and the clothes on their backs. For hardly ten years they had enjoyed the fabulous palace they had obtained by burning a great forest and butchering its inhabitants.*

In Assam, in the Garo Hills, it was the Garo people burning their own forests, ironically. Irawati writes that the Garo, Khasi, and other hill people did not consider themselves Assamese, and with the Central Government's attitude and the missionaries' encouragement, this separation was fragmenting Assam into people who saw only their differences, and not what was common among them. Her minute observations about the land, conservation, and the politics of ethnic diversity in Assam are tragically prescient. The title of her essay is 'The Beginning of the End'.

~

During her stay in Assam, Irawati was told over and over that she had to be always cognizant of the presence of elephants. She was pleased when she first heard this, she had a great love for these wonderful animals. When she was in South India, in Kodagu, with Anand and a niece and nephew as assistants, they had lived in an elephant camp. They had seen how wonderful these creatures were, how loved and how well treated there. There was a vet dedicated to their care, a perpetually worried man who explained that those were precious animals, and their well-being was more important than anything. The elephants, too, were gentle and loving and most mild-mannered. Once when an elephant was thought to have injured a person, the person was immediately assumed to have been the culprit. 'He must have done something to the animal,' the people around said, 'he should be in jail.'

On one occasion in a temple near Mysore, the elephants were dressed up in gold ornaments and decked in flowers. She saw several priests and people around them, feeding and fawning over them. Irawati laughed at the spectacle. The elephants probably thought the songs were being sung for them.

So it caused her great consternation when she heard that the elephants in Assam were extremely dangerous to humans. They would attack anyone they saw, she was told, and if they had vehicle trouble on the road at night, they should just abandon it, because the elephants would crush it into dust. She thought this could not be. She had to find out for herself if this were true, and if so why elephants here acted like rabid animals. Her inquiries revealed a cause that was obvious and simple, and also sadly predictable. Many of the hill people had guns, and used them on the elephants. A bullet usually did not kill these big, thick-skinned animals, but it did cause immense suffering. Elephants are social creatures, and the memory of elephants is no myth. Once attacked by humans, they all know throughout the population, as well as across generations, that humans are terrible, the enemy, and to be attacked at every opportunity.

Irawati saw many contrasts in Northeast India and the South Indian states—like the way the two ends of the country treated their elephants, and the forests they lived in.

~

Jai accompanied her anthropologist mother on several occasions. She went to Travancore, and also to Odisha and Bihar. She had a different experience from Anand. She travelled with her mother to very remote areas, sometimes walking many hours a day to get where they were going. On some trips she remembers being driven to villages, and that there were always people waiting to receive them wherever they went, and interpreters when they were needed, because Irawati had arranged everything by letter before departing on her trips. Things did not always turn out as planned though. Sometimes Irawati would be stranded at remote bus stations without anyone arriving to receive her, sometimes there was nowhere to stay but a barn or the back of a truck, and too often there was no food. She told Jai that her role model was the camel. Eat as much as you possibly can when food is available, and draw on your stores when it is not.

In Odisha, Irawati wondered why this once fertile and rich land with thriving trade ports and shining cities, a university from ancient times (Nalanda) that gave the world great Buddhist and Hindu poets and writers, had now become a poverty stricken, disease-ridden, forgotten-looking land.

Leprosy and black fever (visceral leishmaniasis spread by sandflies) were common, as were occasional massive floods. But these things were also common before, as the oldest history books record. She thinks that perhaps she knows the reasons why: during Mughal and British rule the land was parcelled off to rich landlords, who were not always from Odisha. Lord Cornwallis,[37] for one, auctioned off huge acreage of Odisha's farmland to wealthy Bengalis. As a result, Odia who had lived on and farmed the land now did so as daily wage labourers for Bengalis who had never set eyes on it. These Odia labourers did not profit from the crop because they didn't own the land, and they soon fell into poverty. Their health deteriorated, and they became prey to the diseases that they would have resisted in times of better health. Education was no longer a priority, and, over the century Odisha became as Irawati found it. Listening to a discussion among young Socialist Party men, she says she could see no sign here of the awakening of the new age of post-independence India.

When she began to collect blood samples, Irawati was asked the usual question: 'Can you tell me what diseases I have in my blood?' She would always answer 'no' but then she would start the conversation with a question of her own. 'Do you think you have any diseases?' In Odisha they told her that there were many diseases that plagued them. She had already seen people everywhere mutilated by elephantiasis. She had been sitting by a small lake one evening watching the sun set. She marvelled at the lotuses and waterlilies of every size and colour that covered the surface, and was moved by the beauty of this land. She heard people behind her, and turned to find, to her horror, that they were all people suffering from leprosy. She asked the Odisha government official accompanying her if there was a leper colony close by, and was further horrified when he told her that leprosy was rampant in Odisha. She found out this was not an exaggeration. Not a single village she went to was free of leprosy. On top of all that, the river water was poisonous—in fact they renamed it 'Manusmara'—killer of humans. She had never, until then, heard of a poison river. This river, they said, flowed through thick forests that were full of cobras, and that was the reason the water was poisonous. When it flowed through that town and met two other rivers it became clean again.

At night, when she and Jai needed to test the blood samples, again, there was no refrigeration, and it had to be done the same day it was collected. Swarms of flies and mosquitoes arrived as soon as they opened the vials, and Jai had to fan them away as her mother did the testing. When it was bedtime, the insects were still hovering for blood, this time theirs. Irawati advised Jai to cover her head completely with the bedsheet. 'Wait. Let me think about whether I prefer to die from malaria or black fever, or from suffocation,' was Jai's response.

On this trip, Jai and Irawati also went to the city of Dwarka. While Jai was bored by the monotonous process of measuring people and collecting blood samples, Irawati was thinking about the rather dismal city of Dwarka as compared with a city of the same name in the Mahabharata. That Dwarka, the city that Krishna built, his embodied consciousness, his embodied dream, a city invincible and beautiful, perished and fell into the sea when Krishna himself perished. Irawati contemplates finding Krishna's city, which in the Mahabharata was swallowed by the sea, and the Jains say burned to the ground. She wonders if they would find signs of the ancient city and the people, like Pompeii after the eruption of Mount Vesuvius. According to Irawati, the city known as Dwarka where she was doing her fieldwork was a deformity, compared to Krishna's great city, symbol of his defeat and downfall, gone now, and one, she says, best left where it was: in history and memory. Her essay is an example of the way she addresses the Mahabharata as if it were a historical document, one to be studied and interpreted, and its characters nothing but people, if not always ordinary ones, people nonetheless: people who drink alcohol and gamble, who love and hate and fight, who are strong, but also weak, and who live, and die, whether they are Arjun, or Draupadi, or Krishna himself.

~

On these trips all over the length and breadth of India, Irawati took blood samples, and she measured the bodies of people—following the anthropometric methodology she had learned in Germany.

Irawati used the anthropometer and other instruments she had brought from Berlin to measure thousands of people. She measured different body parts—arms, legs, nose, forehead, head shape, the whole-body stature, etc. She would measure and read the measurement numbers out loud, and her children-assistants would note down the numbers. They also catalogued descriptions about people's eye shape and colour. Irawati measured some women, but most of the measurements by far were performed on men. This was because, she explains, women were more prone to resist or shy away from having their heads measured (when they wore a veil or other headwear) and in some cases women observed the practice of purdah, rarely exiting the space of their homes. There are other instances she recorded about people protesting or complaining about being measured and examined, or having blood taken from them. Some women in a village in Odisha, for example, were unhappy, and winced when their fingers were pricked and then squeezed for a drop of blood. On other occasions, men, too, were less willing to comply with the measurements because there were rumours that those sampled would be enlisted into the army. Another rumour going around was that blood was being drawn for vampires!

Measuring body parts of thousands of people produced, of course, thousands and thousands of numbers. After fieldwork, these numbers were computed, and with them, the anthropologist versed in statistics could produce an average number for a group of people. With that at hand, and with the help of some 'ideal types' photos, one could imagine or visualise what an average or 'normal' member of this group would probably look like: the shape of a person's head, nose, height—these and other body parts took form in the anthropometrist's calculations and imagination.

But Irawati not only compared the bodily differences between the people and their social groups. She also tried to learn something about the ancestries of the different castes and ethnic groups whose members she measured. This sometimes led her to unexpected, original conclusions concerning the origins of the incredible diversity of peoples in India. One conclusion was that the different groups of Maharashtrian Brahmins were not necessarily more similar to each other than they were to other castes, like Marathas, that lived in geographical proximity to them. This conclusion might have sounded scandalous for the caste purists. Building upon this fact that different Maharashtrian Brahmin groups were rather biologically dissimilar to each other (and more similar to other upper castes in their vicinity), Irawati put forward the thesis that subcaste (or jati) differentiations were a product of a lack of fusion between jatis—and not a product of fission of one bigger caste rank group (also known as varna).[38] This means that, according to Irawati, Chitpavan Brahmins and Deshastha Brahmins, for example, might have each had a particular history of ancestral migration to, and group formation, where they live now, not necessarily sharing a common ancestry just because they were both labelled 'Brahmins'. The varna system with its four-caste rank differentiation (Brahmin, Kshatirya, Viasja, and Sudra) is, for Irawati, rather an ancient theorization, or just a model to explain social differentiations, and not an indication that all groups under one varna shared common ancestral origin.

Irawati's anthropometric research had other political implications. One important political process her research supported was the creation of the state of Maharashtra. Before Maharashtra was actually a state, with her anthropometric research Irawati painted a numeric image of what distinct 'Maharashtrians'—Adivasis, inland and coastal Brahmins, Marathas, and so on, in the greater area where Marathi was a common language—looked like, also showing how similar they were if compared to other Indians living outside of the imagined borders of that yet non-existent Indian state which would be called Maharashtra. Irawati's physical anthropological work on Maharashtra supported the idea—which she was also in favour of—that the Marathi-speaking region should separate from the Gujarati-speaking parts of the Bombay Presidency and become its own state, Maharashtra, which finally happened in 1960 following bloody political turmoil. Many of Irawati's publications on the cultural and biological uniqueness of Maharashtrians helped the argument that these people should have a regional state of their own.[39]

This speaks of the power of physical anthropology. Matching a kind of body, or a kind of face, to a culture, a geographical area or political entity (like a state or a nation) has had impactful consequences, not only for the good but more than often for the worse. While the linguistic nationalisms in post-colonial India made use of anthropologists' research on the anthropometrics of a region—putting such research to work for the redrawing of inner regional borders—at other times the nationalism that accompanied the imagination of the biological shape of the humans forming a nation was less unproblematic. Joined with racial methods and theories, biological nationalisms have often essentialized differences between people and excluded specific groups of people. Those with faces or bodies that did not match the expected average face or body of their neighbours often suffered the consequences of being excluded from the political territory they actually belonged to. The questions of where someone is from (the origin question) and who belongs where (the inclusion question) are essentially about political power.

The anthropology produced in Nazi Germany provides the most tragic example of the dangerous consequences of racial essentialist thinking in science. Asking why someone is different produced 'scientific' methods that ultimately created difference in a way that produced, and created, 'race'. If anthropometry was mostly used in anthropology to measure 'others', in post-1918 Germany, this method of measuring body parts was increasingly used on the 'others within'—like the Jews and Roma and Sinti, which were minoritized groups in German society. German anthropologists' increased attention to these othered groups followed from Germany's loss of its colonies at the end of World War I, which meant that German anthropologists also lost their easy access to faraway places where they could do research. The result, as Nazism progressed, is known. Measuring faces—especially noses—was also used in contested cases to determine whether a person was Jewish, and German anthropologists, including some of Irawati's colleagues in Berlin, did this kind of assessment for the Nazi state. In many cases, these anthropometric assessments, however frail methodologically, had tragic consequences for the measured person: deportation to an extermination camp or fugitive exile. Anthropometry in (and often supportive of) this context of hyper-nationalism and violence, would have genocidal consequences. The result of applying state power to work for racism was death on an industrial scale. This explains why, after World War II, scientists around the world have increasingly distanced themselves from this method. Not only was the method considered unsound, but, throughout the decades following 1945, the whole idea that 'race' was a biological entity capable also of influencing culture or behaviour, was discarded. This turn away from 'race' was a development that Irawati would also experience and reflect on, perhaps realising that, after all, the idea of 'race' and racism are intrinsically interlinked.

11

Zugvogel

Irawati did more than collecting blood samples and measuring bodies on her field trips. In fact, these field trips were also key to her social and cultural anthropological research and informed her most known books in the academic world, like *Kinship Organisation in India*. Given the incredible diversity in which different peoples around the world conceived their relations to their relatives and kin, kinship was a focal area of social anthropological research at that time. Therefore, Irawati was especially interested in understanding how people would name and organise their family relations. And understanding kin-making in India inevitably touched on the question of caste. Caste was a topic of international interest in anthropological theorisation and for which Irawati dedicated many years of research and countless pages of writing.

To understand the different kinship practices and terminology, Irawati used any and every contact she had—with colleagues, but also family, friends, acquaintances, students, government officials, and of course, the people she met when she went out into the world. She would start with the one person she had established contact with, and then, through them another person or family and another—like a hippie hitchhiker, she went from one village or town or to another. She would get into a crowded bus, or a crowded third-class train compartment which were, she says, opportunities she sought for collecting kinship material. She would talk about herself and her life with the men and women she met, and they in turn told her about themselves. She couldn't always whip out her notebook in these places, but she writes that she took down '...Kinship terms and situations involving personal narratives or family usages, scraps of song and proverbs.'[40]

By comparing kinship patterns, as well as blood groups and physical patterns of variation, she strove to understand the diversity of languages and ethnic groups in India, how they came to be what they are, their relations to other groups, now and in history—which could be traced back to ancient times. She explains:

> *When there was not material for measurement the time was spent in canvassing contacts and there were never enough funds or time to do this type of work for more than two months a year. After coming back to Poona the data would be looked into and verified linguistically by referring to some good dictionary and then a study of some literature would be undertaken to find out how far the literature reflected the kinship attitudes. These studies were very rewarding. They revealed the intimate connection between literature and social, especially the kinship organisation and helped to interpret certain facts which had seemed obscure to me. Such studies also gave a feeling of sureness while dealing with people.*[41]

When on her field trips, Irawati ate and slept wherever she could. She found that people were generous, and took her into their homes. She found this work immensely rewarding, though her days were long and there was never enough money, because it brought her closer to what she felt was her life's work: *to understand who we are.* As much as scientific methods and theories have changed, this big question forms the central concern of the whole science of anthropology. And even though this scientific field has grown and branched out to study many different matters and concerns, including much more modest questions, Irawati was moved by this big question, by all the mysteries of human life in its incredible diversity. Her pursuit of answers to this profound interrogation as well as her curiosity about the culture, language and society reflect her life-commitment to the science of the *anthropos,* the human—and her holistic approach to it.

~

In trying to understand the whole of the diversity of shapes, ways and meanings of human life, Irawati, like most anthropologists, often also focused on small bits of this whole. Like most anthropologists, she also did specific long-term studies of some ethnic groups, such as the Bhils in Madhya Pradesh and the Dhangars and Nandiwalas in Maharashtra.

Most people in Western Maharashtra have seen a Nandiwala. These nomadic people would go from village to village offering consultation with their oracle, which was a bull. People needed important questions answered, such as if their crop would thrive, whether their child was male or female, whether a family member would recover from an illness. Nandibail—the vehicle of Shiva—highly decorated and well-trained, would reply with a 'no' by swaying his head from side to side, or a 'yes' by nodding it up and down. The Nandiwalas were paid for these consultations with cash, or in kind, with grain or other items, as they went from one place to another. In the late 1960s, there were between four to five hundred families that made up the Nandiwalas. They were an accepted and familiar part of Maharashtra. Irawati studied them to understand a particular aspect of India: the Nandiwalas were a living example of a group who had relatively recently migrated from one state to another. Understanding them and their experience of moving across regions would help to answer the questions: with whom do people identify when they migrate? How have groups migrated across long distances in the Indian subcontinent—in the recent and ancient past? How have they adapted to the new place and society, how were they received? How did social status and caste rankings play out in such migrations?

The Nandiwala families travelled in small groups, they travelled through rough terrain and slept in jungles and on mountaintops, and they hunted along with their trained dogs catching small wildlife that included hare, iguana, pigs and deer. Every year, the families gathered on a large field on the outskirts of Pune. Here they would stay for two or three months, and perform all their social rituals—marriages, naming ceremonies—and also settle their disputes. It was here that Irawati sent her students, B.V. Bhanu and K.C. Malhotra, to establish rapport with the Nandiwalas, to introduce their interest in researching with them and get their permission to do so.

The Nandiwalas' headman was a tall and imposing gentleman in a turban. He had agreed to give them an audience, and was told that the anthropologists would spend time with the families, and ask questions, and observe the Nandiwalas for several years, even following them on their journeys. The man listened with some impatience and then asked, 'But who is your headman?'

'Dr Irawati Karve,' they informed him, and hearing this the headman demanded that he would only make a decision after he had spoken with this headman.

As requested, Irawati, Malhotra, Bhanu and several students arrived the next day to meet the headman. The camp was rife with activity, and a rather unpleasant smell: it was the day the Nandiwalas slaughtered several pigs. They would be skinned and cooked and the meat would be sundried into strips of jerky. This was carried as backup in case they received no food and were unlucky on the hunt. The sensory output of the camp that day was difficult for Irawati's students, many of whom were lifelong vegetarians. They felt uneasy.

Irawati talked with the headman, while the others stood at a respectful distance. The discussion seemed friendly, and the headman was clearly pleased with Irawati. They chatted for some time. Then the headman called out to some of his people. A man went away, and returned with a large platter. At this point Irawati immediately turned to her group and said in English, 'Do what I do.'

The headman took the platter, on which lay several pieces of partially cooked meat surrounded by watery and pinkish looking liquid. He held it out to Irawati. The woman that her students called 'sir' took a piece and put it in her mouth. The platter then went to the others in the group, who dared not do otherwise, in spite of their normal diet habits, their religion, or even their preference at that moment.

The headman then instructed his people that they would cooperate with whomever Irawati sent to them, that there would always be a tent available especially for them, for as long as they needed. Malhotra, then a young lecturer, became Irawati's first PhD student.[42] He went on to follow and study the Nandiwalas for several years, and wrote several papers on them. This group of nomads—who were actually quite wealthy, who were money lenders apart from their bull-oracle activities, who settled their own disputes without the use of courts and who distributed all the wealth equally among themselves in a sort of socialist way, who killed a particularly evil member of their family (Ram Mama) and then deified him, who were regularly possessed by spirits and gods—also gave insight into another aspect of Indian culture. The original question, of whom a social group identifies with when they migrate, was also studied. The Nandiwalas, originally Telugu speakers, who were sixth in the caste hierarchy of their native Andhra Pradesh, became bilingual, and rose up the ranks to third place in the caste hierarchy in Maharashtra, after several hundred years of their migration.

The Nandiwalas, among whom the greatest crime was abusing a mother, the abuser punished by being tied to a pole without food for three days, who were, if not actively feared by the general public, at least sent a frisson of uncertainty through most people, allowed Irawati's students and colleagues to study and accompany them for several years. It was considered a major breakthrough into the community, and all because Irawati spoke to them as equals and ate the food that was offered to her, meat that was at once an offer of friendship, and a test. Bhanu, who was a student of Irawati and remembers this incident, believes that, if Irawati had refused the meat for any reason, they would not have been allowed into the Nandiwala community.

~

On the flat hilltops beside the ghat roads, men in enormous once-white turbans, sometimes with a brown dog or two by their side, herding flocks of sheep and goats were once a common sight. Living in Western Maharashtra, these men and their families are Dhangars—traditionally nomadic sheep and goat herders. They were considered one of only two purely nomadic people of Maharashtra; they worship their god Khandoba, shear their sheep and weave blankets, and wander their strongholds, the stony wastes in the higher region of the Western Sahyadri mountains. The Dhangars were another group that Irawati thought warranted study. From one end of India to the other, nomads who tend cattle, sheep, geese and pig, camel herders, and some who are hunters, travel most of the year. 'They travel with their families and their pets and all of their belongings, and sleep under the stars. They beg a little, steal a little, and work a little,' Irawati has written. 'The foolish agriculturist, with backbreaking work, creates wealth which lies unfenced and unprotected for them to steal from.' If her idea of the nomadic life sounds romanticised, or perhaps overly generalising, it comes from a deep knowledge of the Dhangars of Maharashtra at that specific time. Irawati, feeling that this community should be studied, asked for a grant from the Ford Foundation in the US, but, in 1967-68 the then President of India, Radhakrishnan, reportedly heard about this and offered the money from the Central Government—five hundred thousand rupees—a quite large sum for the time.[43]

In the concluding chapter of her book *Hindu Society*, Irawati makes a plea as an anthropologist 'that we as worshippers of many gods, we find a way to for these nomads to live as they choose…', a statement that shows her anthropological take on the world, which is guided by not only a political commitment to cultural minorities but also a profound sentiment that different ways of life—nomadic or not—are possible, worth living, and worthy of dignity. Such sentiment can be felt in many of her writings. Her essay about the Mahar community and her experiences and feelings about them is an example.

Irawati spent some time measuring and collecting blood from the Mahar community. This group belongs to the so-called lower castes of Maharashtra once called 'untouchable'. Irawati already had a kind of admiration and affection for this community. She was curious about what their origins might be. There were no villages she had encountered without a Mahar community. Mahars would take any work they could get, from being nightwatchmen to picking leaves and rolling beedies, to construction. She observed that they tended to spend their hard-earned money on nice and aesthetic things, little luxuries, which, to Irawati's amusement, aroused the jealousy of white-collar people from the so-called higher castes. Mahars in Irawati's observation were always nicely dressed and cared about being fashionable (her Brahmin students, on the other hand, were usually the worst dressed in her classes!).

The Mahars that Irawati encountered were always immensely curious about what she was doing and why. When she convinced them that she was not recruiting them for the army for a commission, they asked her endless questions. She had a method that she had used on other groups that she had studied. She would hand them an English anthropology textbook. This always silenced further questions, and she could get on with her work. When she tried this with a Mahar man who was interrogating her, he threw it on the table and said, 'Don't you think you should write it in Marathi for people like us?' Irawati knew he could not read Marathi either, but he knew the book was in English, and of course he knew why she had given it to him. She felt she deserved his response. After that she answered him patiently, giving an anthropology lesson to those Mahars who were illiterate but astute and knowledge-thirsty.

Her assistant for this work was one of her students, who was himself a Mahar. He was taking notes and details, and asked the man next in line for his caste. 'Harijan'[44] the man replied. The student became angry and said to him, 'Say you are a Mahar, man. Don't use that word. Be proud.' Then he turned to Irawati and said, 'We are Mahars. Our culture and history is in this name. This Harijan word is one of fake sympathy and pity that we don't want.'

That night, walking back to where they were staying, Irawati and her assistants and students came across a group of men singing together quite beautifully. Irawati stopped and listened. Then she asked them what the song was, and had a sense that the singers felt she should have known it. It was the ballad of Ambedkar. The others with her said she should not speak with the Mahars. She did speak with them, as well as took their measurements and collected their blood and ate with them—Irawati never followed the rules of 'untouchability' or paid them any heed whatsoever. On the bus there she had heard people talking unhappily about 'Ambedkar's man.' He was a Mahar candidate for the regional elections that he would probably win. The Congress Party was spending a lot of money to defeat him, but they knew they had no chance. Irawati said nothing, but was secretly pleased.

Irawati ends her essay[45] on the Mahar community with an incident: on the final day of that trip there was a discussion about where the border of Maharashtra lies. One person said, 'They speak Hindi across that river,' another said, 'Half the people in that village are Hindi and half Marathi.'

The Mahar man said, 'Where Mahars live—that is Maharashtra.'

~

It wasn't just humans and human society that fascinated Irawati. In an essay in the collection *Bhovara*,[46] she also writes about the great delight she feels when swallows and swifts, who, on their quest to find food once winter stilled the insect life in Europe, arrive in Pune. She yearns to see a golden oriole each year and is thrilled when she spots one in the trees outside her office window at the Deccan College, and astounded when she sees flocks of them in Odisha. She welcomes birds with the same joy that she feels when the Dhangars pass through the bustling city of Pune as though it were the countryside. They block streets and traffic with their flocks on their way from the dry plains to the verdant ghats. She had felt this thrill when the sky over Berlin filled with cranes—Zugvögel—migrant birds—flying south in winter.

When she witnesses all this movement, all these migrations, she feels those eighty-four million creatures and forebears, all nomads and wanderers, coursing through her blood. 'People think, there goes the lady on her research trips,' she writes. 'Little do they know.' This is another side, perhaps, to this woman who everyone in academia knew as a passionate researcher. But her great love of wandering is very clear in her essays. Her mind wanders as much as her body: she discusses philosophy, plants, language. She admits that she is obsessed with words. The words for rivers in various languages, she says, say something about the rivers in their country. 'Fluss' is appropriate in German because German rivers flow silently—like the whispering Spree, the silent Rhein, or the elegant Elbe.

'Nadi' is appropriate for Indian rivers, especially the ones that originate in the Himalayas, and, squeezed between walls of rock, roar so loud that it is impossible to hear yourself speak. She writes simply, and yet with so much passion, about everything she sees on the road, and nothing is more important than any other thing—from a tiny common swift on a telephone wire, to the ranks of the Himalayan peaks touched by the setting sun as she struggles to encompass their infinity in her puny human self.

In one essay, she writes about sitting on the edge of Lake Tanganyika, and describes the formation of rift valleys and lakes. She was on a side trip with other academics—palaeontologists and other anthropologists—from a conference, possibly somewhere in Europe. On September 17, 1955, Irawati was on a plane from Cairo to Paris, and then homeward, when she described the land below, and concluded that the Tapi and Narmada rivers too may be in a rift valley, and would be interesting to study.

It was this, Irawati's unbound curiosity and boundless delight in the world and all in it, her deep fascination for the enchantment of life, that drove her scientific mind and imagination.

12

Paleolith and Microlith

In 1929, when Irawati came to the end of her time in Germany, Dinu came to Berlin before she left it forever. The two of them, who had been married two and a half years and had not yet started their life together as a couple, started it there, in Berlin. With the money that Irawati's father had given them to make up for his refusal to support his daughter's Berlin sojourn, they travelled in Europe by train and got to know each other a little—or the new versions of themselves after such a long time apart. The only archive of their trip is a crumbling album of photographs. They are small, and somewhat indistinct now, faded to shades of sepia. But the images, some of Irawati in a German-romantic style—leaning on a grassy hill, standing by a lake, silhouetted at the mouth of a cave or a tunnel—along with views of Berlin, Leipzig, Lake Constance in Southern Germany, Prague, Paris, Venice, with captions in Dinu's careful cursive, tell the story of their late honeymoon through Europe. At the end of the trip, they boarded a steamship back to India. After the excitement of their reunion and their adventures, this journey home was so long, and apparently also so dreary, that Irawati and Dinu embroidered a whole tablecloth together.

Treasured objects, objects that carry history within them, objects that tell stories—even such objects, the most important of objects, are lost. But sometimes, a thing resides in the memories of those who saw it and knew what meaning it held, beyond its function. Irawati and Dinu's tablecloth is known to all their children and grandchildren, not all of whom have seen the object. Perhaps one of them has it, somewhere. Perhaps, when it is found, in the distant future, this object will be reunited with its story, like the objects Irawati herself found in the layers of archaeological pits, whose stories she told.

In 1939, when the Deccan College in Pune reopened and Irawati joined its staff, she was thrilled about the new job: it was an important position, at a time when the college—and India—had the scent of a promising future. A decade after her doctorate, she finally arrived in an institution where she sensed that her scientific career would have space to unfold. She was full of hope about the future—teaching and doing research in fields that were so dear to her—sociology and anthropology, and fuelled with courage that allowed her to forget the challenge of being the first woman in India to occupy such a position. She started as a lecturer in the sociology department. Years later, at the insistence of her students and colleagues, Ramchandra K. Mutatkar and R.K. Gulati, she created and headed the department of anthropology, where she would work for the rest of her life. Although she later stopped teaching to devote her time to researching and writing, initially, when she was the only sociology lecturer at Deccan College, Irawati taught all the courses herself—at least four, and some semesters as many as eight.

Irawati's first year at Deccan College was also the first year of another colleague, one who would work closely with her. On August 17, 1939, Hasmukh Dhirajlal Sankalia disembarked at the Pune railway station. For the sum of one rupee, he rented a horse carriage for the day, and in his own words, 'entered the vast portals of the Deccan College with its magnificent Gothic towers'[47] to begin his new job as a Professor of Proto-Indian and Ancient Indian History.

It was not long before Irawati gave him George Grant MacCurdy's *Human Origins: A Manual of Prehistory*[48] and asked him to teach the course in European Prehistory. At first, she was relieved to have Sankalia as a colleague to whom she could pass on some of her heavy teaching burden. And there began a relationship between two intellectuals, two characters so unlike each other that they should not have gotten along at all, a peculiar and close relationship that would last her lifetime.

The Gothic building that Sankalia so admired was the Jeejibhoy castle, where both Irawati and Sankalia had their offices, only a few steps away from each other. They both took those steps whenever they felt the need to consult with one another, which was often. A person walking into either of their offices might find, at any time of day, the two deep in discussion. Irawati, for whom the world was a whole that included the physical past, the detritus of bodies and belongings, was deeply interested in archaeology. The discussions and learning from each other between Irawati and Sankalia took place in their offices in the Gothic castle, as well as on their long, sometimes day-long walks along the shores of the Mula-Mutha rivers in Pune, where they would go together to find the past in the layers of soil and rock on the riverbanks. It would carry on in train compartments and buses when they travelled away from Maharashtra, up to the Gujarat desert, where they made startling discoveries together. It would continue in the evenings after a day in the pits looking for the stone tools and bones of ancient people.

These archaeological expeditions were large productions. Although they usually made arrangements before their arrival for places to stay, they had to take a cook and all the equipment he would need. Large steel trunks containing their pots and utensils, plates and kerosene lamps were part of their kit, as well as bedlinens and blankets. They would buy rice or wheat and vegetables at the local weekly markets, but on occasion even had to carry those when they were going to a particularly remote area. When this party—with cook, assistants, photographer with his paraphernalia, surveyor with his, Irawati—a fair-skinned, tall woman with no signifiers as to her status and yet clearly one of the leaders of the group, and Sankalia with Mrs Sankalia, also a confident and unusual woman—arrived in a village or town, there were times when they were mistaken for a travelling circus or theatre troupe and were refused lodgings until they convinced the person in charge of who they were.

Irawati and Sankalia were very different from each other. Gujarati, devout Hindu, great believer in astrology and a lover of mystery and unexplained phenomena, Sankalia was born very sickly and not expected to live. Much to his mother's joy, he did, but was a slender and frail adult with a delicate constitution, and a particularly fragile digestive system. Irawati, Maharashtrian, who experienced religion in an almost intellectual way, who thought of herself as a scientist, who was tall and imposing, and, until her heart betrayed her, was a healthy, even vigorous woman. She had walked miles and miles for work and pleasure. She swam when she could. Before her diet was restricted later in her life, she ate what she liked, and also whatever she had to without any negative repercussions on her digestion or constitution. Sankalia recounts an incident in his autobiography about how this discrepancy between them had a terrible consequence for him at an archaeological site in Langhnaj in Southern Gujarat where they had made an important discovery together:

> *Iravati Karve was so much pleased [about the discovery] that she thought of celebrating the occasion by offering me a glass of lemon juice. This did not agree with me not being accustomed to cold drinks even on a very hot day. Next day I felt sick and had an attack of diarrhoea and I was completely run down. And though vomiting stopped, the diarrhoea continued. With great difficulty we reached Pune. The weakness in my legs too continued for months. And I wondered whether I would be able to do any field-work at all. However, a course of ematine injections restored my health.*[49]

Fieldwork did require a strong stomach at the best of times. Irawati herself often had to eat whenever and wherever she found a meal, and when she didn't, she had to improvise it. On one of their many expeditions together in Langhnaj, the two of them decided to go on a side trip together to nearby Hirpura, where Sankalia had stayed for a few days in 1941. They took two workers with them, the rest of the party stayed at the Langhnaj site. When they got to Hirpura they realised that no one was willing to put them up or feed them, because one of their Langhnaj workers was a 'semi-untouchable.' As a result, after the journey, Irawati had to rustle up a meal for them, which she managed on a makeshift stove with wet firewood.

There is a passage in Sankalia's autobiography that touches on so many aspects of his and her relationship. It gives a sense of the difficulties that came their way in their quests to find clues about the unknown past, and it also gives insight into Irawati from a person who knew her well, and who had a long and layered relationship with her.

> *As I have said in the preceding pages, my health being what it is, I can ill afford to take liberties with my food or drink. Even an extra cup of tea, I had to refuse when offered on numerous occasions by our hosts. On one occasion when after a long walk from Hodol we reached Dharoi, late at night, with our camp followers and equipment, we found to our great surprise that the only place where we could stay, a school room, had been closed for the week-end. We were advised to find shelter in a garage on the river bank. Unfortunately there was a truck inside the garage which carried kaolin from the local quarry. So some of us had to sleep in the truck, and others lay under it. As it was already quite late our cook gave us what he could cook in a trice which turned out to be khichadi, a melange of pulse and rice. I hesitated. Dr Karve, who was a hard taskmaster and a dour disciplinarian hurled a lecture at me. When she did not stop for some time, I quietly remarked, 'Dear Mrs Karve, don't you know, that you are a paleolith and I am a microlith.' This was the most apposite simile that I could think of, for in every way she was different from all of us. But I never imagined that this remark would sting her like a thorn. It haunted her that whole night and for many years which I later on came to know when I narrated this incident to M.C. Burkitt, the doyen of British pro-historians who had invited both of us to lunch at his house in Cambridge in 1951-52, Dr Karve then said, 'Your retorts are very painful. They directly*

> *hit at one's weak spot.' Dr Karve was right because two of my ruling stars are Sagittarius and Scorpion (sic).*[50]

~

Sankalia's office was typical of an archaeologist. There were trays laid out on white cloth-covered tables. They held finds from previous trips to Langhnaj. He worked on the pottery fragments, microliths, paleoliths, bone fragments, and an assortment of various items whenever he had the time. Irawati, always particularly interested and curious about Sankalia's work, walked into his office one afternoon as she sometimes did, and began to browse through his trays. He was used to this, and continued his own work.

'Is this from Langhnaj?' she asked suddenly, rather quietly, and he, hearing something in the quaver of her voice, answered, 'Yes, everything there is from the Langhnaj site.' He saw that she was examining one of the bone fragments.

'What is it?' he asked.

'This is not animal, Sankalia, it is human,' she said. Her eyes were shining, and she was clearly quite excited. This was her area of expertise. She knew human bones when she saw them, and he knew this. He knew her training in anatomy and physical anthropology in Germany, under Eugen Fischer. He knew what this might mean.

And so, a year after the first expedition, with funding from the government and the University of Bombay, they had returned to look for remains of those humans who had used those tools, and who had eaten those animals, in the Mesolithic Period (10000-8000 BCE). As Sankalia says in his autobiography, they had come looking for humans—Microlithic man or Mesolithic man, but certainly, the oldest man in India.

On the train going north, to Gujarat from Pune, on yet another journey away from home, Irawati thought about how time seems to collapse between two similar points. It felt to her that it was just the other day they were on this same train, when in fact it had been a year ago.

When they arrived at their destination the station was deserted except for the people who were there to receive their party. Irawati could see the people they had worked with the previous year. They were standing behind the iron perimeter of the station, all waving and shouting excitedly. There were ten or eleven people, and Irawati felt like she was an old friend, or family member, being welcomed back by nephews and nieces.

Soon, the mountain of bags and boxes they had brought—far too many for the small group which had alighted from the train—was loaded onto some cars. The smaller articles were carried by members of the welcoming party, and by Irawati, her colleagues, and the cook. The place where they would stay was close to the station, and they began to walk.

Irawati had this odd sense of repetition, but not quite. She thought about déjà vu, but it wasn't that either. It was just what she had thought on the train: the time between these two visits had somehow telescoped, and the illusion that she had experienced nothing in the year that she had been gone from that place persisted. Time was complicated, and not always linear. Memory played with it. Memory and emotion took it into loops and warps that changed one's perception of it, that brought long gone moments close and disturbed the straight lines of happening. She shook it off as tiredness, and began to prepare her mind, as well as the physical and practical things, for the days to come. There were four people to a room, in a small bungalow. This was where she would rest in the afternoons, and sleep at night, where she would keep the few belongings she had brought with her—books, toiletries, clothes. One corner of a room, for a little over a month. Irawati would share the space with her assistant, a student, and the photographer. The other room was given to Sankalia, who was the leader of this trip, and his assistant, one student, as well as the surveyor. Mrs Sankalia was not with them this time. There was no other woman among them. This was not surprising. Parents of unmarried women and husbands of married ones would not let their wives or daughters, if in fact any had made it to graduate level at university, travel so far from home for so long, in the company of men. It was February of 1944. Irawati herself had left her youngest child, Gauri, who had just turned two years old on the eleventh of that month, to come on this archaeological exploration. Dinu was at home in Pune to look after her, as well as Jai and Anand, who were not yet in their teens.

Irawati thought of Southern Gujarat as an ocean of sand. She was unused to this terrain, in spite of the weeks spent here before, she dreaded trudging through the sand, feet sinking in at every step, every step plunge and retrieve and plunge again. Shoes filling with the sand, getting heavier, heels rubbed raw the first days, blistered till the calluses formed. But though everyone suffered, they all knew that but for this plush blanket of sand preserving what lay beneath it, they would not have found the signs of a human settlement, fifteen thousand years old. In 1943, at this very site, they had found stone tools and bones of animals the humans must have consumed, but they had found no human remains at all. Or so they thought.

Even before choosing the site, marking the search areas, and beginning the process of moving vast quantities of sand, the preparation work would begin the following day. A carpenter and an ironsmith would come from the village, to sharpen the pickaxes and shovels and fit them with wooden handles. The team employed people from the village to do the actual excavation—several men to scoop up the sand, and women to carry the sand away from the site. Irawati and Sankalia, who were the senior members of the team, sat together and made lists and assigned roles, discussing every detail. They and the others unpacked their own tools. Meanwhile, water was heated for their baths, and when it was ready they washed, one by one, in the single bathing room, cleaning their skin from the heavy desert dust.

The bungalow was at the edge of a lake, and easy chairs lined the long open verandah, where the party sat and waited for their evening meal. One by one, people from the village began to arrive to see them. These were people they had met before, and Irawati, though tired from the journey and excitement of being there, was pleased to take part, and also listen to the gentle chatter. Sankalia spoke with them all. He spoke Gujarati, and though Irawati understood and could speak, she was not fluent.

One of the visitors, a teacher, said, 'We are so grateful that you are here again.'

Another person nodded. 'Important people such as yourselves, visiting our poor village…'

Then, a wrinkled fellow quite a lot older than the others said, shaking his head, 'What is all this about 'grateful' and 'important'? People will go where their fates take them, where their food and water take them.' He seemed irritated by their obsequious comments, and had a different point of view.

'Yes, yes, that is true,' the teacher agreed. 'After all, would we even meet each other, but for the entanglements of our past lives?'

Irawati heard his words as if in a dream. As the sun set, the village, the tops of trees, everything before her turned to gold. The lake was liquid gold, its surface shimmering in the mild breeze. And as she watched, the gold began to take on the reds of the sunset, and she heard a familiar, and unfamiliar sound, a yearning crooning call that brought back memories of another, quite different place. Sarus cranes flew in over them. Irawati was always moved by nature, and particularly by birds. She passed her deep emotion for these, the winged co-owners of our earth, on to her children, and her grandchildren. She wrote about the cranes she saw on that day:

> *Just as I thought it was the time for birds to come home, my enthusiastic ears were rewarded by the harsh, but yearning call of Sarus cranes, and then a pair flew past the bungalow toward the lake. They flew low, their ashy blue wings spread wide, their long legs stretched behind them, maybe two or even two and a half feet long. Their equally long, rounded necks tapered to the point of their beaks. Midflight, they called, 'Krrr, Krey,' and beat their heavy long, wings.*
>
> *'Just like planes,' one of us said, and I shook my head, no. Not at all. The flight of planes didn't compare to this living beauty. All the components of planes are tight, unmoving against each other. The wings of planes sit permanently at the same angle to the fuselage, their flight is lifeless, a product of human invention. But this pair of cranes! The tight stretched neck-leg-wings, fluttering momentarily, then beating heavily, this flexible, living organism, this proof of living will spread ripples of joy through my mind. The pair made slow circles and then alighted at the shore of the lake. They*

> *set down in tiny little jumps—so as not to burden their thin legs all at once, before standing still. They seemed to decide, speaking their usual 'Krrr, Krey' sounds, to go into the lake. They lifted each leg high, and softly put it down into the water, like a person stepping in gently, so as not to splash the water onto their clothes, just like a woman in a saree. More pairs of Sarus arrived, calling, 'krrey krey.' Peacocks on the tree right before us began to call, 'myaow, myaow,' and soon birdcalls filled the air.*[51]

On such missions the days began early, they tried to get out and be at the site before the sun became too intense. Though it was winter, the bright light directly on them in the shelterless open sand could be harsh. They had a tent and water and food, and they took breaks. But it was physical work. They had marked out the two areas for the dig on the previous day, and though the men they had hired from the village had the job of digging and the women of carrying the actual sand from the dig area, Irawati and Sankalia and the others on the team had to be there, and supervise their respective teams.

The first day, old man Hiraji, de-facto leader of the village team due to his age, picked up his pickaxe. He would make the first strike into the ground, ritually, to start this enterprise auspiciously. Hiraji swung his pickaxe high behind him, and shouted 'Jai Bhavani' to invoke the goddess's benevolence upon their enterprise, and the pickaxe arched through the air and struck the ground. Then the work began. Each pit would be sixteen feet by six, measured and marked out by pegs hammered into the ground. Quite soon stone tools and artefacts were unearthed. They were photographed and catalogued, and taken away to the tent. Irawati was deep in her pit when she heard them calling her from the other pit.

What followed is best told in Irawati's own words, from her Marathi essay. In it she recounts the events of February 28, 1944:

> *I climbed out,* [of the pit she was working in] *and my assistant came running up to me and said, 'Hurry, they've found a human skull,' and I ran over, excited. Inside the second pit, I saw a rounded yellowish object peeking out of the earth. I moved everyone away, and with a pick and small knife I carefully loosened the dirt and released the object. It was a large, smooth, yellow stone. We hid our disappointment behind laughter and went back to work. I went back to the first pit grumbling about people calling on me to dig out pebbles when I found the workers there sitting with a big lump of earth.*
>
> *'Look, this time it really is a skull, and we thought it was a stone!' I looked, and it really was, stuck there in the earth, a human skull. I sat with it and began to work on it, with picks, knives and brushes, to clean it off, and all the rest of the company gathered around me, watching.*
>
> *Everyone at the camp had assigned jobs. The artist/ photographer and the surveyor drew and photographed the pits and the objects, and they made maps. Our chief* [Sankalia] *supervised everyone, but mainly, he was the expert on prehistoric stone tools. I had done much study on human skulls and bones, so any time human remains were found, I was put in charge of them. While I worked at clearing the dust and debris off the skull I reported details to my colleagues.*
>
> *'You see here how the skull has been pressed by the weight of the earth on it? The joints of the skull have*

come apart, and there are cracks in it.' The skull belonged to an old man. He would have lost his teeth while he was still alive, and his tooth sockets had closed up. His lower jaw, due to the loss of the teeth and the wearing away of bone, had narrowed. Unfortunately we didn't find any more of him. We decided it would be better to photograph the clean skull right away. Not far from the old man's skull we found a complete skeleton. This man had his arms placed across his chest. His right hand sat at his left elbow, and the left hand at the right elbow. His legs had been crossed. The most astonishing thing about it was the huge crack in the left side of the face, from his forehead to the chin. It was a clean blow that caused it. The bone was cut through, and the passage of millennia did nothing to quell the frisson of fear in every witness' heart. The man was young, 25 or 30 at most. Even the labourers were stunned. Into the silence old Hiraji said, 'Bai, he must have died in a war,' and everyone was somehow relieved by his words.

One of the young assistants said, 'Yeah, right, the young man died in a war, and his old father died from grief.'

I made eye contact with Sankalia and both of us began to laugh.

The following day, not very far from the two men, we found the remains of a dog.

'So how did the dog die,' everyone wondered. The dog made things clear. He had not died of natural causes, he had been killed by a blow to the head.

I told them, 'Probably, a man died in this settlement, and his tools and property were buried with him, and his servants, and his faithful dog, have been killed and buried with him too.'

Everyone agreed with this assessment, and we got to work with greater enthusiasm.

My body and mind was only partly on the job with the others. Unlike the previous year, though we found many artefacts then, I was affected deeply by these incredible revelations of ancient society.

I worked with the assistants, to carefully remove the skeleton with its layer of earth intact from the ground, to layer it in wax, to wrap it tightly in long strips of burlap, to then encase it in cottonwool, to place it in a trunk. But my mind wasn't on it. I felt as if I was trying to see through a deep winter fog that would part momentarily, reveal something vaguely familiar, and then close up again. I stood on a hill and looked around at the oceans of endless sand spread around us. The lake lay like a mirror-smooth circle, without the slightest wrinkle of a wave on its surface. The sea is never smooth this way, those tiny waves are always present, even when it's calm. Those waves spread out on the ocean of sand, in the direction of the wind. But, unlike the restless, ever-moving waves on the ocean, these waves lay still, fixed. I was in fact standing on the crest of a wave—a dune. The sand was alternately shallow and deep, and I could see the next crest of a sand wave rising beyond the one below me. These dunes must have stood this way for tens of thousands of years. This dune I stood on must have been just the same, perhaps smaller, because fifteen millennia of sand had collected on it since. Those primitive people lived here then, they had drunk water from the lake, and, and...? The fog had parted for a few seconds, and I thought I saw a familiar face. But it was gone again, veiled again in the fog. I was in a state of gloom when I slept that night, body and mind as though exhausted.

I woke with a start, there was some disturbance, I could hear my name being called, but I was frozen in some unknown fear. The commotion got louder, I would have to go see what it was. I went to the door, touched the latch, and a shaft of lightning illuminated my body.

'Who is it?'

The familiar voice of Sankalia brought me out of the fog. My legs were unsteady, my mouth was dry.

'It's me,' I said to him, 'I'm just going to step outside a minute,' and I stepped out into the veranda. It was bitterly cold, I shivered. I drank a sip of freezing water from the terracotta water pot outside. The water froze a path from my lips to my belly, dispersing the last of my sleep. I was completely awake, conscious. It was dark, a bitter cold night characteristic of southern Gujarat. The clear deep sky was crowded with bright star points. All of creation was silent. I rubbed my eyes and took a deep breath. I felt as one does after a long hard cry—my throat hurt, my chest was heavy. I couldn't remember why I had awoken, nor what dreams had disturbed me. I went back inside and lay down to sleep in my corner.

It was two days after, when 'she' was found. The leg bones came free first, and we suspected human remains. We put the labourers at a distance and worked with small tools around the perimeter of the bones to expose and free the skeleton whole. I had had a feeling from the moment I saw that leg bone. And now I was sure.

'Since that dog I've felt we'd find a woman, and now here she is,' I said.

'Does this mean she's been murdered too?' my student asked me.

'There's no doubt,' I said. 'Just as he needs his servants and faithful dog in heaven he needs his wife too, don't you think?'

'Are you sure this is a woman?' they asked me. 'How do you know?'

I explained it to them all—the smallness, the lightness of the hip bones, certain characteristics of the skull—and when this lecture was finished they all stood. Sankalia had instructions for me.

'Look,' he said, 'this skeleton is now in your charge. The sun is too high right now, the light will be better in two hours or so, before sunset, for photographs. We're going back to the other pit. You get it ready by then, right? Do you need any help?' I said I didn't, and they all went back to their work. I was alone in the pit. The sun was beating down hard. I bent over the skeleton and cleaned it carefully, with a pick, a small knife and a brush, without disturbing a single bone. Those bones were seeing the sun after being blanketed in earth for fifteen thousand years. This woman, like the man, was buried with her arms across her chest, legs bent, turned on her side. But unlike the man, who spanned a large space, she was so very tiny, she took up only a tiny space. I cleaned out all the bones of the body and my hands turned toward the head. It was such a tiny head. It seemed so delicate. My mind took notes like a machine as my fingers moved on her smooth skull.

'The back of the skull is distended, the forehead somewhat narrow.'

> *My pick worked on the eyesockets, and they were soon clean.*
>
> *'The nose bones, the nostrils below, they seem wide. The nose would have been squat and broad. The cheekbones are small.'*
>
> *My hands were at the jawbone. The bone was yellow-black, just like the earth. But when the brush touched the jaw the teeth were exposed, they shone in the bright sunlight. My heart was thudding. I could hear my colleagues' voices as though from a dream.*
>
> *'Wisdom teeth are not seen, she was very young,' my mind noted mechanically, automatically. But my conscience was filled with a fantastic restless fervour. I saw pupils moving in those eyesockets. I saw those teeth shine in a smile of recognition. My fingers were engaged in the work of cleaning that narrow tapering jaw, but my heart spoke to this pile of bones, 'Are you me then? Are you me?'*[52]

This is not the first or last instance that Irawati talks or thinks about rebirth, about previous lives. It is a subject that seems to run through her mind, and even bring her comfort in times of uncertainty, especially in the dark moments when her life did not seem long enough to do the work she wanted so much to complete.

Irawati observed the people above and beneath the ground, she went to the strange places her thoughts took her. In Langhnaj, sitting in a pit with the bones of a woman dead fifteen thousand years, Irawati was an archaeologist, a forensic pathologist, a historian, an anthropologist, and a philosopher. And she was a woman who was inspired, not by the discovery of the oldest *man* of the subcontinent that Sankalia was so eager to find. It was the remains of a *woman* that inspired her philosophical explorations about time and existence.

13

East and West from the Thames

Irawati stood on Waterloo Bridge and gazed at the peculiar sight reflected in the Thames. The fabric of the night sky over London had a huge rip in it, letting in an almost painfully bright light from the other side of the universe. In the daytime, this tear in the sky was actually an enormous and beautiful metal pod which seemed to her an engineering feat. Three hundred feet tall, suspended fifty feet above the ground with no apparent support, she could see it even from great distances away. It was lit up at night, creating that wonderful illusion of an opening in the firmament. Whether intended or not, this sight felt like a metaphor to her, of the hope and expectations, the desire to rebuild the physical space and the minds of the people of the city, and the whole country, recovering from a brutal war whose origins she had seen in Berlin, whose aftereffects were all around her, there in London. The Skylon tower was part of the Festival of Britain. London was trying to be cheerful, festive for the festival. She didn't feel entirely like a stranger because she actually understood what she heard on the street. This made her at once at ease and uneasy—she was no longer a citizen of the Empire, but she would always be one in so many ways. English, after all, would always be her language.

The feeling among all those she met and talked to was one full of hope, and the Festival of Britain made it more so. But underneath all that there was scarcity, poverty, and like it had been two decades ago after another war in another city, people bore visible and invisible scars of what they had been through. It was 1950, five years had passed since World War II had ended, but it was not so long that things were normal, if they would ever be again.

Irawati had been invited to the School of Oriental and African Studies (SOAS) of the University of London as a visiting lecturer and guest scholar. It was special too, to be there as a free citizen of a country that, until only four years before, was part of the Empire. She herself had always felt that the British Empire was a kind of Anglo-Indian collaboration—that Indians, despite colonial rule, basically ran their own country. She wondered if that was the reason why the transfer of power was, when the time for the long-sought independence was ripe, relatively painless compared to many other countries that became free from British rule around the same time as India.

This time at the Port of Bombay when Irawati had boarded the passenger ship *Stratheden*, she was forty-six years old. She was leaving Dinu behind again, and this time also her three children. Jai and Nandu were older, and probably did not miss their mother as much as she missed them. But Gauri was not yet ten when she left, and would be by the time Irawati returned home. Dinu, yet again, was left with the care of the house and the cats and dogs, and though Jai and Nandu did not need their hair combed and shirts buttoned or help with their homework like Gauri did, Irawati had no doubt that they would all be well looked after.

Although Irawati was in a place where the language

was her own, she was still, as she was in Berlin, a stranger away from home, and she was lonely. There was rationing in England, but it didn't affect her terribly. She was used to simple food at home, and she had lived in Berlin as a poor student. When Irawati was invited to dinner parties at Oma's house, she had noticed that the potatoes served there were always peeled and in perfect cubes that could only have come from the centre flesh of the potato. She wondered what they did with the rest of the tuber and its skin, and it seemed like a terrible waste to her. Now she could see the other side of that. Nothing was thrown away. Mashed potatoes were mashed whole, centre, sides, skin and all.

The Festival of Britain wound down. She had seen all the exhibits more than once. The bright floodlights on building faces, beam lights on fountains, and spotlights everywhere were suddenly turned off. The Skylon Tower, suspended over everything like a fresh anchovy, was dismantled and vanished, leaving the sky dark. The waterfront, once quite cheery, went back to what she supposed was normal. It would not have seemed that way to her if she had not seen the festival lights, but now it was desolate. That first winter there, London was beginning to remind her of Berlin more and more, when some trees lost all of their foliage as though overnight with one chilly gust of wind, and it began to feel as if the earth no longer revolved around the sun, so little did they see of its light or warmth. London didn't have much sun anyway, even when it wasn't fall or winter. There were no shadows at all, the muted, gentle sort of light that came through the perpetual cloud cover created no contrast. Compared to the light at home, where sunlight and shade were two different worlds, where drops of bright sun fell through leaves onto dappled dark earth and made a pattern like the stars on her saris, where all colours glowed and sparkled in the harsh daylight, and birds and people alike searched for the shady side of the street, here it was all pastel and smooth. No one colour was brighter than another. And then there was the fog. This was not like the fog at home either, that sprawled in Himalayan valleys or crouched under city bridges and vanished with the slightest touch of morning sun. No, this fog was a creature of the coal dust that hung in the air from all the factories and home fireplaces. It was a ghostly embodiment of the soot that coated the buildings of London in a suede blackness, that made old and young lung-sick, that she could wipe off tree barks with the palms of her hands, darkening them so that she could never wash them completely clean. It would appear every so often, and then people would fall, cars would crash, even ships on the Thames would collide. This fog, so thick that it was said to have thwarted Hitler's attack on the city.

King George VI died in February while she was there, and the coronation of the young Elizabeth was to be in the following June of 1952. Preparations included washing the buildings clean of the soot that coated them, and Irawati was astonished to see the buildings that were washed revealed to be white, standing next to those as yet unwashed, still hidden beneath layers of coalblack.

Irawati was fascinated by all that was London. She loved walking, especially through the parks, and doing that alleviated her loneliness. From Kensington through Hyde Park to Saint James was five or so kilometres, and she took her time to appreciate the trees, and the ducks and swans on the lakes, and watch the people. She found the English landscapes, in the city and the country, most pleasing. Even in autumn, even when it was bleak. When leaves fell like rain from the trees that still had them, people would come and sweep them every evening, into neat piles by the roads and paths. At dawn they would set fire to the piles, and despite the choking smoke that hung in the already sooty air, it was a beautiful sight to her. When all the leaves were gone, the trees stood like skeletons, but under them, the grass was as green as it was in the summertime. This was a quintessentially English thing to her. And she knew why it was so.

One day, walking home to Camden street from work, her neighbour said to her, 'Why, you are soaked,' and Irawati, surprised, ran her hands over her long beige wool coat and touched the scarf covering her head and realised that yes, they were completely wet. The English rain, she thought. And walking through the soundless incessant humidity, she understood Shakespeare's words about the quality of mercy. It didn't fall, this rain, it was just there. Always. It kept the grass green in the fall, and it gathered around the coal soot in the air sometimes, making the fog.

Irawati occasionally attended an English professor's lectures on Indian classical music. She didn't care much about what the man said, it was more because he played a phonograph record after his talk, which she loved to listen to. Once he spoke about the raag Malhar, the rain bringer. As he put a record on his machine, he said he didn't really understand the connection between this raag and the rain. Irawati understood at once. This man, who had never been where rain comes like a passion, all sound and fury and torrents and thunder, could as much fathom the connection between Malhar and the rain as she could a mercy that 'droppeth as the gentle rain from heaven.' She knew now, what that was. And why the grass was green when nothing else was.

Irawati also understood now why British paintings did not have a clash of colours in either the landscapes or the people—pink, flaxen-haired, pale-eyed. She writes in her essay 'Malhar'[53] that she wondered when there would be an artist who would paint, for example, a woman she once saw on a rocky slope in Maharashtra, a woman carved out of that very black rock, in a bright green saree, her eyes dark like that same rock but polished, she was so beautiful that Irawati's breath stopped, and she never forgot her. It wasn't that she didn't find the people in England attractive. She did. She enjoyed looking at those pale pink, golden-haired, blue-eyed men and women too.

Begeisterungsfähigkeit—German for the ability to feel enchanted, to feel enthusiasm for things in life—is a word that defined Irawati in her wanderings in the world. Even though she was not always happy, or at ease, the world poured into her. Trees, birds, people, their clothes, their ways, their talking, the past and present, every detail—she was never bored, because she was open to it all. On the worst of days, the British Museum was only a short walk from SOAS, as were other smaller museums. British philosopher Jeremy Bentham was one of the founders of the University that the SOAS was a part of, in 1826, and someone Irawati found fascinating. Bentham's dead body, preserved as he had directed, had been sent to Stanstead Bury, to keep it safe during the war, but had been returned to London in 1951, to the university, so of course she went to visit him. The essay[54] Irawati wrote after her encounter with Jeremy Bentham's auto-icon is an example of the fabulous entities that flew out of Irawati's mind—a wild planted and carefully nurtured, ever-expanding, botanical garden of knowledge.

What came to Irawati on seeing Jeremy Bentham in the flesh was an ancient story from Kalidasa about a lion whose job it is to protect Parvati's tree from destruction by animals.

One day, King Dileep of Ayodhya, who has for various reasons been temporarily assigned the care of a cow, wanders into the area. The lion, hungry and tired, wants to eat this cow. The king explains to him that the cow should be spared, and the lion should eat him instead. The lion in turn explains to Dileep that he is the king, and is needed by many more people—his family and his subjects, who look to him to rule them and provide for them and keep them safe. 'The good of the many,' the lion says, 'is more important, so you should not be the one I eat. This cow has just one calf, and it may survive without her.' But the lion is a decent character, and Dileep convinces him that he should eat neither of them. The story continues about how King Dileep and the cow go on to live great lives and so forth.

At this point Irawati always fretted about the lion. Kalidasa never mentions him again. What happened to this poor creature?

In Irawati's version, he must have died of old age, or worse, of starvation. And having died thus, unfulfilled, he would have to be reborn. After waiting centuries and centuries, he is finally reincarnated in England, to the Bentham family, and he is named Jeremy. Irawati has called her story 'Absolute Proof of Rebirth'—Jeremy Bentham's philosophy, she says, is known in every corner of the world: *It is the greatest happiness of the greatest number that is the measure of right and wrong.* Which is exactly what the lion was trying to explain to Dileep. Not only that, but the lion, as Jeremy Bentham, was reborn in a cow-eating place, where he could eat beef to his heart's content.

~

Sankalia was in London briefly. It was a city he knew well, from his time as a PhD student at London University. His visit, including a luncheon with him at the home of historian M.C. Burkitt in Cambridge was a welcome distraction. But eventually, the darkness and gloom did begin to affect Irawati. She was losing her motivation because of the lethal combination of the weather and her loneliness, and when people began to chit-chat about their Christmas plans, she became depressed. None of the people she worked with and had become familiar with thought of asking her what she was doing over the Christmas-New Year period, not her colleagues, nor any of the students. But though she felt sad, and even upset, Irawati need not have worried.

At SOAS Irawati worked on what would be one of her most important books: *Kinship Organisation in India.*[55] In 1951, a certain Austrian count by the name of Christoph von Fürer-Haimendorf became the Chair of Asian Anthropology at SOAS. Having spent the decade before his return to London (1949) in the field—in the far northeast of India among Naga people and the Gonds in the south among others, he had a profound knowledge of those areas, but also of the country in general. He was always available and willing to discuss even the smallest points of doubt Irawati had. He gave her access to his own data whenever she needed it—for example, with the Gonds and Kolams of Hyderabad, on whom he had done years of research.[56] From Irawati, he in turn, learned about all things Maharashtrian. But even he, one of the few people who cared about her work, was ambivalent about what she taught her students. None of her other colleagues seemed aware, let alone curious about her at all.

Given Irawati's declining mental state, the work that she had intended to do at SOAS was beginning to stall. Her feelings of isolation in the vast city—and the impending winter—were taking its toll on her ability to carry on doing it. She was beginning to think that *Kinship Organisation in India* would never be completed, let alone published. There was, however, a personal angel in London for Irawati, in the form of Elizabeth Haimendorf. Professor Haimendorf was no doubt immensely helpful to Irawati in her work, but it was his wife who recognised that Irawati was struggling in other ways. Betty, as she was known to everyone, was herself a well-known anthropologist, and one, as Irawati writes, 'whose knowledge of Indian anthropology is very great.'[57] Betty Haimendorf was the moving force for her husband's field work. She made all the arrangements, financial and practical, for him, and also, wherever they went, they went together. She was invaluable to him, with her willingness to go anywhere, and her ability to be warm and kind to whomever she met, be they from her own upper class British society, or people of the high Himalayas. It was this same supportive, concerned, generous nature of Betty's that came to Irawati's help when she needed it so much. Irawati became dependent on her willing and easy-going friendship and straightforward, heartfelt support. She says of this relationship, 'At times I despaired of ever moving forward with the book and would certainly have ceased writing it but for the constant goading and ready help of Betty Haimendorf whose friendship for a lonely elderly Indian woman in a strange city was even greater and more useful than the former.'[58] Irawati in her loneliness (thinking of herself as 'elderly' when she was not even fifty years old), valued Betty Haimendorf's friendship even more than her help with her work.

So many women have unstintingly supported their academic husbands and male partners, even making possible careers and works that might otherwise not have been possible. This was also the case in anthropology, a discipline that, for example, connects the invention of its main method, ethnographic fieldwork, to one Bronislaw Malinowski, whose work, nevertheless, would never have been possible without the help of his wife—the writer and journalist Elsie Masson—even though he (and most of his biographers) gave her so little credit.[59] So many of these women went unacknowledged by these men over the centuries. Irawati's acknowledgement of her friend Betty Haimendorf is, therefore, especially important, and is also an example of women in academia supporting one another. This remarkable duo of intellectual women—Irawati, with her star-printed sari, and Betty Haimendorf, with her eternal cigarette—were responsible for the first draft of *Kinship Organisation in India*.

It was no surprise then, that when Christmas was upon them, it was with Betty and Christoph Haimendorf that Irawati celebrated. Their house was full of mementos from their travels. Christoph Haimendorf has taken more photographs of the people of Northeast India than anyone else—a record of lives that no longer exist. Some of these were displayed on the walls. He had a huge collection of opera records—he was Austrian after all, and in fact went to Vienna every year to attend performances. The Haimendorfs were generous in spite of the rationing and shortages. They hosted large and small parties in their home and garden, and Irawati was one of their regular guests as long as she lived in London.

~

How do the castes and ethnicities of India keep themselves apart and distinct from each other? And how do they interact, under which rules and patterns, and how do these distinctions and interactions keep 'Indian society' together and functioning? These were some of the questions Irawati addressed in what became the first book that granted her international recognition, *Kinship Organisation in India.* The lively intellectual exchange in British anthropology was decisive for Irawati's approach in this book. This was the heyday of social anthropology in its structural-functionalist accents, a tradition of thinking in anthropology that was mostly concerned with how a society is organised and keeps its social order. This social anthropology school thrived in Britain—also due to the open routes to, and political and economic interest in all the faraway places of the British Empire. After Malinowski, this tradition was further enhanced by the theories of Alfred Radcliffe-Brown, who, after doing fieldwork on the Andaman Islands and many other places, was the first chair of social anthropology at Oxford University, a position that was followed in the late 1940s by Edward Evan Evans-Pritchard, who continued to develop the theories of structural-functionalism. Also based in Oxford at that time was sociologist-anthropologist Frenchman Louis Dumont, who was also an India expert. He was one of the many peers with whom Irawati had discussions about her work when she was in London.

This intellectual landscape was an incentive for Irawati's further distancing from the racial anthropology that she had learnt in Berlin. While that Berlin school of physical anthropology had taught her to measure bodies to make inferences about different peoples (or 'races') and their history, the social and cultural anthropology she immersed herself in London reasserted her intuition that biology is not the ultimate realm that explains humanity and human differences. This led her to write, in concluding *Kinship Organisation*: 'Culture is not a thing dependent on physical heredity but ultimately a culture walks on two legs.'[60] Overall, the book presents a mix of approaches and methods that are distinctive of Irawati's holistic take on anthropology, reflecting the patchwork of intellectual traditions she took inspiration from. One of the book's chapters is devoted to an analysis of ancient epics and religious texts, while others look at sociological aspects of caste and ethnic differentiations in India, at the same time that her earlier anthropometric research still informed some of the book's comments.

Also because caste, including India's societal organisation based on the rules of caste, has been an insightful theme for social anthropology in that structuralist-functionalist tradition, Irawati's *Kinship Organisation* found a lot of resonance within the international anthropology community.

While Irawati was in London, the Assistant Director of the Rockefeller Foundation, Chadbourne Gilpatric, became interested in Irawati and her work. He met with several people in Pune about her work, and heard that she was 'Ghurye's best student'. Gilpatric, who was not able to stop in London, then invited Irawati to Paris to meet and interview her. After this meeting, he wrote his impressions of her in his diary. His observances contain clues to Irawati's state of mind, but also, as their later correspondence reveals, hints at the beginning of a long association and friendship. Gilpatric wrote:

> *In view of Mrs Karve's many interesting ideas on value formation in India and the composition and changing features of its contemporary culture, I said I thought she would have several interesting suggestions for interpretative work on India of first importance. This*

> *would be of interest to us in the Rockefeller Foundation and to others like* [American anthropologist] *Cora Dubois and other leading students of present-day Indian culture. I suggested that she consider a short visit to the U.S., which would be her first, en route home to India early in the summer. It would be necessary to have a formal request from the Deccan College, and funds needed would cover travel, living expenses and a small allowance for her family. She is anxious to get back to Poone* [sic], *but sees several advantages to discussions on Indian problems worth studying with interested Americans. She will spell out some of her own ideas on paper, and if a travel grant were made, she would prepare notes for circulation to a few selected Americans before she arrived in New York. She is a deliberate person and does not want to move about just for the sake of travel or seeing different places. It would be useful to discuss her work and possible visit with Kluckhohn*[61] *and others at Harvard.*[62]

Gilpatric also notes in his diary that 'Louis Dumont, now at Oxford for three years, who has been working on social structure, especially the family in Tamil Nad [sic], has much confirming data for Mrs Karve's hypotheses. Professor and Mrs Cristophe [sic] F. Haimendorf in London are helping with her writing and enthusiastic about the implications of some of her hypotheses.'[63] It is even more surprising then, that on publication, Irawati's book would receive a demolishing criticism by Louis Dumont.

After their meeting in Paris, Chadbourne Gilpatric was convinced that Irawati was an exceptional academic, and Irawati received a grant from the Rockefeller Foundation to present her ideas and meet with American academics, a kind of scholarly tour across the US, from New York City to San Francisco.[64] Her obligations at SOAS ended, and Irawati took TWA flight 963 on June 29 to New York for the two-month-long trip. The Deccan College agreed to extend her leave for this period, and requested the foundation to pay her salary (Rs 400 per month), which they did. There was a not entirely positive attitude among her Deccan College colleagues—murmurs of discontent that made Irawati nervous enough to write to Gilpatric about it. Also, after nine months in London, she was anxious to go back home. In spite of this, America was good to her, as she wrote in a personal letter to Chadbourne Gilpatric:

> *I had a lovely time at Cornell and Chicago. At Cornell I was very happy indeed. I talked shop with Professor Opler*[65] *and his colleagues and felt refreshed and rested in the beautiful campus in spite of the overpowering heat. I got more out of my few days with the American University teachers than 9 months with the English. In fact the two experiences do not stand comparison. I was in England for over 9 months teaching anthropology but not one co-teacher asked about what I was doing. They were simply not interested.*

Irawati's journey back, several flights and layovers, took four days, and would today be considered a nightmare. But she didn't see it that way. To her it was the beginning of a love affair with America, where she would return many times in the future.

~

In *Yuganta*, Irawati writes:

> *From childhood to death the one thread that creates the oneness in a man's ever-changing life is smriti.*
>
> *Smriti is the power which enables a man to have the ever-present consciousness of who he is and the knowledge that he is the same person from moment to moment. It is because of smriti that a man understands what his duties are, and where he is going. In the Mahabharata the question 'Who am I?' is bound up with the question, 'What is my place?'*[66]

Whether she first encountered these questions in the Mahabharata or not, 'who are we and how did we come to be the way we are' are questions that Irawati asked herself, questions the anthropologist exists to answer. Irawati, in her unfettered vision of the world, looked in earth and stone, body and blood, song and text, for answers. One of those texts, and perhaps the most important of all the texts that Irawati turned to, was the Mahabharata.

On her sixty-first birthday, Irawati received a gift from her father: the Bhandarkar Oriental Institute's nineteen volumes of the Critical Edition of the Mahabharata. This work, the result of the labour of many, many scholars comparing all existing ancient manuscripts from the different countries and several cultures this ancient epic has percolated into, had begun when Irawati was fourteen years old. But she had known this epic for as long as she could remember. Many Indian children know the stories within the Mahabharata before they know of its existence or that it is the source of all these tales they have heard from parents and grandparents, read in comic books and seen in countless retellings in films, TV series, plays, dance dramas—it is a thread sewn into the patchwork quilt that Irawati likened Indian society to, if not one of the main threads that holds together a sense of cultural identity of the country, sometimes even across religions and beliefs. It is no surprise, then, that Irawati recognised the Mahabharata not as a work of fiction, but as a historical resource replete with details about the lives and times of a people, not just in the times of the Mahabharata, but in the present of the Indian subcontinent. She saw that other thread that the Mahabharata is—running through not just the cultural identity of India, but the historical one: a kind of smriti for a whole people. It is perhaps so accepted into the consciousness because it is that. Irawati does not see the other Indian epic, the Ramayan, as well known and also part of Sauta[67] literature along with the Mahabharata and the Puranas, in the same way. Irawati turns to the Mahabharata again and again as a source for insight into the society of ancient India, one that also helps to understand present Indian, and specifically Hindu culture, religious practices, beliefs, and the meaning of human existence in ways that no other historical document can. To her, the Mahabharata was so real in its historical depiction of ancient Indian society, and therefore today's Indian society, especially in the north of India where Sanskritic languages are spoken, that she used it to actually illustrate family structure, relations, and kinship.

Irawati's anthropological and historical reading of the Mahabharata caused controversial debate in academic circles. Her biggest critic was none other than Louis Dumont, the French anthropologist who had acquired fame as the most referenced name in the study of the Indian caste system.[68]

In London, while working on *Kinship Organisation in India*, she even exchanged letters with Dumont, he being at the time a lecturer in Oxford and having done some research about one caste group in India. Dumont must have engaged considerable time and interest in this exchange with Irawati—she was even careful enough to thank him in the acknowledgements in the book. But surprisingly, although *Kinship Organisation* received some very positive reviews in prominent journals,[69] Dumont did not spare bitter words of criticism when he wrote about the book. His hostile review came out in the first edition of a famous journal for Indian sociology, and, in fact, as one of Irawati's biographers noted, 'The reputation of *Kinship Organisation in India* never quite recovered from the *demolition job* performed by Dumont.'[70] The French scholar seems to have been annoyed by the fact that Irawati did not undertake extensive fieldwork in all areas covered by the book (India)—which would have been impossible, naturally, and especially given Irawati's limited budget and time to cover the whole country—and he wrote, in a somewhat sarcastic tone, that Irawati must have felt 'self-assured' in her 'birthright' to write about India just because she is an Indian national.[71]

Seen from today's perspective, there is sweet irony in Dumont's sour criticism: In 1966, years after the publication of Irawati's book, he would publish his most famous book, *Homo Hierarchicus*, which intended to be a generalising account of the caste system for the whole of India. The book essentialized 'hierarchy' to be the organising principle of Indian humanity, the *homo hierarchicus*.[72] Dumont, of course, did not do fieldwork in the whole country. In fact, his work has been criticised for relying far too much on just a few informants of one Brahmin caste group.

But what bothered Dumont the most in Irawati's approach was the attention she gave to the Sanskrit epics and how she mixed history and anthropology, often interpreting anthropological data in light of historical and textual sources. He claimed that her approach was not 'the proper anthropological attitude' and questioned if the book was scientific or 'modern' enough, or if Irawati followed rather a 'Hindu, Brahmanical method'. Dismissing Indian anthropologists for the simple fact that they were Indian—and thus, by his logic, not objective enough—was an attitude that Dumont would repeat some years later in another controversy, one that other famous Indian anthropologists would question and write about.[73]

Indian anthropology is still haunted by the ghost of Dumont, a European armchair scholar who became a gatekeeping and iconic figure in the study of caste and Indian society. This story also demonstrates a pattern of injustice in the way science works internationally—those scholars located in Europe or North America usually having the most authority in theorizations about the global South. This unfairness in international scholarship is something that Irawati, too, noted. Years later, when she wrote about being silenced in academia (she was brushed aside by European scholars when a younger version of herself tried to compare caste with forms of social stratification in other societies), she notes, perhaps with a resigned smile, that Dumont's work received special praise for his comparison between India and the West. He was lauded for his ambitious but rough parallels between Indian and Western values, as were American writers for comparing caste in India and race in the US,[74] something Irawati, and other Indian scholars, had already done.[75]

But Irawati always remained convinced of her approach of considering literature and history when studying a present-day society. She explained:

> *I myself started my enquiry as a field-worker and turned to the written records only when I could not understand some of the data I had collected and found that the written literature helped me to understand my field-notes. Words which I had taken down without understanding their full significance became clear when I found them in the context of a story or in a poem. Usages which had appeared strange to my urban upbringing could be placed in their proper setting and perspective when found recorded…A people's literature has a peculiar relation to their social institutions. In some kind of literature the social institutions are idealised, in another they are ridiculed; in a third the literature is starkly realistic. All the time a particular type of evaluation of social institutions is found in literature and I found this interrelation of the written or oral literature and the actual social institutions as lived by people a fascinating study in idealisation, rationalisation, self-castigation, self-criticism, suggestion and imitation on the part of a society. The cultural lag between the literary norm and the actual conduct is itself a study of enormous value and for such complicated cultures as that of India as essential as field studies.*[76]

The future of anthropology would agree with Irawati, giving her much more credit than Dumont did. Taking a position diametrically opposed to Dumont was American Indologist William Norman Brown, who created the first department of South Asian Studies at University of Pennsylvania, as well as the American Institute for Indian Studies (where Dinu served as director after he retired from teaching). Brown has pointed out that precisely because Irawati was Indian, and also because of her study of 'pertinent material in Sanskrit and allied literature from the time of the Rig Veda' few investigators can present what she has.[77]

The decade following Irawati's death year saw much discussion and some turns in anthropology. In the 1980s, both the 'writing culture' movement and feminist scholars made a lasting plea for more self-reflexivity, something Irawati always did and shared in her writings many years before, making her an easy target at that time for men like Dumont who thought she was too subjective. More recently, the so-called 'literary turn' in anthropology made anthropologists engage more seriously with literature, making literary culture a trending topic of research.[78] To the dismay of Dumont's ghost, anthropologists today are reconciled with historical and textual methods, bridging the present with the past, the lived with the written. In the second edition of *Kinship Organisation*, Irawati wrote a remark about, or to, the 'average non-Indian anthropologist', perhaps in response to the famous French anthropologist of India:

> *I found that the average non-Indian anthropologist knew very little of Indian literary traditions and sometimes did not care for them either. To him this appears as a useless, nostalgic dipping into a vanished past. I assure him that that the past lives with us even today vividly, obstinately and sometimes obtrusively and must be known by everyone interested in the present.*[79]

Maybe just to be sure that her point comes across (or to teach the less-informed European audience), she made sure to include a summary of the Mahabharata in the appendix of the revised edition of her book.

~

Irawati knew that without Dinu, neither the book nor any of her life, particularly her academic life, would have unfolded the way it had. Betty and Christoph Haimendorf, who both acknowledged each other's role in their achievements, may have influenced her heartfelt public acknowledgement of this fact, and also how much she missed Dinu during her time in London. Her words of thanks, to Betty, Christoph, Dinu, and many others named and unnamed, are also acknowledgement that intellectual achievements are rarely those of a single individual alone, and that they reflect a network of exchange, support and care behind them. This is especially so in anthropology: Irawati says as much in her essays about her field trips to gather all that data that fills her book, that it would have been impossible without the people who told her about their lives, experiences, knowledge, fears and hopes, and also, welcomed her into their homes and families, and were generous with not just their stories, but shelter and food, and priceless access to their social networks.

The first page of *Kinship Organisation of India* reads:

> *To my husband*
>
> *While dedicating to you this book which would never have been either thought out or written but for you, let me express my feelings in the traditional Hindu manner:*
>
> *I place my head on your feet and ask for your blessing.*[80]

14

Edge of the World

It would be spring soon, the spring of 1959, in beautiful Berkeley, California. But Death was stalking Irawati, he felt like a second shadow, one who didn't need light to exist. Day or night, he was her companion, and, she realised, he was one who had always been with her. She just hadn't noticed before. In spite of all the evidence—the knowledge we are born with, the knowledge we gain, the woman in the sand dead for fifteen thousand years, the skulls and bones Irawati had held in her hands, the parents and friends, teachers and students vanished into the eternal answer to all questions—in spite of all of this, we live as though we will live forever. We ignore this companion who is always with us all. When the fog rolled in and out again over San Francisco Bay, and the sun hit the water just so, making it shimmer and dance, she understood, or remembered, for a moment, that Death was a good companion. He sharpened her focus on life, he opened her senses, he reminded her that every sight of the Pacific, every autumn day and summer night there in the far west at the edge of the world, was the only one. This moment would never return, and no moment ever does. Death, then, became, every so often, her friend. She had no tricks to play on him or special things to show him. She could be the best or the worst of herself, and he would still want her.

The house was not big, but it was roomy. It was comfortable, with large windows, trees formed a green cocoon around it. They had arrived there, Irawati and Dinu and Gauri, months after leaving home, and this would be their home while Irawati worked as a visiting professor at the University of California at Berkeley. In Europe, her inexplicable fatigue, breathlessness and chest pains had finally been diagnosed as a heart condition: Angina. In spite of this, Irawati and Dinu did not return home. Her condition, though she felt it that way, was in fact not immediately life-threatening. The university, informed of the new situation, made arrangements. There were two nurses waiting for them at the house, and as soon as they got out of the car they sat Irawati down on the large sofa and took her vitals, and drew blood. Irawati was exhausted, and had not said much on the drive. Gauri had vivid recollections of that journey. She spoke incessantly, pointing at everything excitedly, and her father laughed and enjoyed her and her childlike enthusiasm. Irawati rested her head against Dinu's shoulder and dozed, each return to consciousness was treated to descriptions of cars, the size and beauty of the actual road they were on, any birds that could be seen at that speed, and only a gasp of utter delight, when the water came into view, and then awed silence as they travelled the bridge across San Francisco Bay into Oakland. Though they were going east from San Francisco, she knew it was the water of the Pacific Ocean. They were at the edge of the world. This then, was the farthest Irawati had been from home in her whole life of travels. She thought about how her mother must have felt. And thinking about the ocean and all the rivers of her life, she fell back into a deep sleep.

By journey's end, Irawati was really drained. The travels had been wonderful, in a way, but not, as she had thought, energising. She had thought the brisk weather in Europe would lift her up. As she lay on that big sofa everything felt like a too-fast movie, a landscape that slipped past the window of a train, moving, moving, gone before there was time to focus on something interesting that caught her eye. Zürich, München, Tübingen, Bonn, Amsterdam, and, after a long blue wait, finally, New York City, had slid past the window, and as she lay there on the sofa in the deepening gloom of their new home, she tried to recall the time behind her. She tried to put the exhaustion, and then the terrible pains that had become her new companion aside, and think about the other things. The new and old friends they had spent time with, the conferences, the universities and institutions she had been invited to. She was welcomed and looked after by people with love and respect at each and every place they went to. Full venues and engaged audiences at her talks and conferences would have delighted her, had she not been so tired, not just from her illness but also from the constant fear that the ribbons of pain would wrap around her chest at any time. She didn't want to be anxious or sad about this new reality. This sense of the precariousness of her body, her life. It was difficult to accept, for her, who had always moved through the world with ease. She had travelled to places where others did not go, places that were physically hard to reach, that were uncomfortable or even dangerous, but she went, because of her curiosity, her desire to answer her own questions, and the questions of the world. The sadness was becoming a part of her, she did not want it to define her. She wished she could accept and live with the things that came with a poor heart: the medications were not many or difficult to take, the restrictions were not ones that particularly affected her—she found that she mostly already ate and drank as a person with a bad heart should. She started taking saccharine in place of sugar, she ate grapefruits and pomegranates, she had never cared much for fatty and spicy foods anyway. But the pain, and the feeling that she was leaning on Dinu, and also the children, that everyone worried about her, that she worried about herself—these things brought with them a kind of sadness. She tired easily, but she could hide that to an extent, and she was able to accept it when someone asked her if she had had enough and would like to rest.

Irawati had settled on the sofa when all the welcoming committee had left. There had been the doctor and two nurses, one of whom had taken the blood sample and the other her blood pressure. The doctor gave her various instructions, and she was glad Dinu had been there to take them down. Then she heard Gauri's voice, she was speaking softly, so as not to disturb her mother.

Irawati sat up and looked around. This was to be their house for the next two years. There was a fireplace, with a log in it, but no way for smoke to go outside. There was a writing table, so delicate that Irawati says it couldn't possibly hold more than a few papers for writing a letter. A piano stood on one side of the room taking up quite a lot of space, but it did not make a sound when Gauri tried to play it. It seemed like a stage set for a Jane Austen novel. The sofa was very comfortable, and Irawati could see the kitchen from where she sat, and it seemed very well equipped with all the modern amenities that an American kitchen ought to have.

Her companion sat beside her in the gloom, motionless, his gaze as ever on her.

'You are the watcher,' she said to him. 'I experience it all, and you, you watch me.'

He didn't blink, just sat there, unmoving, ever-present. She said, 'I like this house. It's a good house to live in. And a good house to die in.'[81]

~

Irawati loved being in California, and she had known she would. On her first visit to America in 1952 at the invitation of the Rockefeller Foundation she had experienced generosity and hospitality from every person she met. Professors and students in Ithaca, Chicago, Washington D.C., New York and UCLA and Berkeley had shown enthusiasm for her and her work. Many of the people she met wrote letters of thanks to Chadbourne Gilpatric at The RF Foundation and expressing their positive feelings toward her. Melville Herskovits at Northwestern wrote to 'Gil' that 'She is a remarkable woman who has done an amazing job on pitiable resources. I hope that you are able to give her some funds'[82]—for a research problem he felt had 'unusual long term significance.' Morris Opler at Cornell wrote saying how interesting their discussons were, as did Maureen Patterson in Washington D.C. She had not seen these letters of course, so she had not imagined the warmth she experienced, nor was it merely politeness.

Irawati had travelled to California as well, and to Arizona, where she fell in love with the land itself. From her hotel room in Los Angeles she wrote lavishly of her delight to Chadbourne Gilpatric: 'I am glad I'm going away soon before America sweeps me off my feet.'

Promising a formal report of her trip, she ended with these words that illustrate how she felt about her weeks in the country: 'In the meanwhile goodbye and a thousand thanks for the last month and what is to follow. Even if my plane crashes in the Pacific I shall die without regrets.'[83]

She was not disappointed by America. In spite of being aware of her body and its new limitations, Irawati found that she was able to enjoy her colleagues, her students, the lectures, and the simply beautiful part of the world that they had landed in.

Her other worry, apart from her health, was Gauri. She and Dinu wondered if they had been wise bringing her teenage daughter, a rather outgoing and curious one, with them. But leaving her behind was just as fraught. She would settle down, they told themselves, when she had to go to class every day and study and take exams, and she would make friends. Irawati herself had not been much older than Gauri was now, when she went to Berlin after all.

Gauri went to the official orientation for new students at the University of Berkeley one morning. She did not know it when she went, but this orientation was not for general students, just for the foreign students who had joined that semester. To the surprise of her parents, she was so angry when she came back home that, as she was to recount later, she could barely explain herself.

'They want me to wear saris all the time, can you believe it,' she said, 'and do you know why?' she asked, and before Irawati or Dinu could answer, she shouted, 'because they don't want us to be mistaken for Mexicans!'

Irawati tried to calm her down, but Gauri was inconsolable in her disappointment. She was right after all, to be angry. Irawati always wore saris, but that had nothing to do with American prejudice, that was just who she was. She liked her saris. They were specially woven for her because she was too tall to be able to wear the ones available in stores, so she got to choose her weaves. And then she had them screen-printed all over with tiny khadi stars, and she wore them with great enjoyment. But it was not the sari wearing that irked Gauri. She was angry about the layers of prejudice involved in such advice, given by the all-knowing and wise administration of the university itself: the lady representing this administration told the bewildered gaggle of foreigners gathered there that if they presented themselves as exotic outsiders, then their experience of racism would not be as harsh, perhaps, as what Mexicans, who worked as seasonal farm labourers and gardeners and construction workers all over California, receive. After the first weeks Gauri refused to wear saris. She wore jeans and t-shirts, which looked alarmingly like men's undershirts to Irawati.

Both Irawati and Dinu worried about their youngest child. Irawati remembered the pregnancy, the birth of this daughter all too well. Jai was already ten years old, and Nandu eight. They thought they were done with babies and small children. And then, in 1941, when Iru was thirty-seven, they found they were to have another child. It was not the easiest of deliveries. Irawati was in the maternity hospital's labour ward along with a few other ladies also in labour, when the obstetrician came and admonished Irawati for expressing her pain as deep moans and long groans.

'Must you do that, Iru? It's upsetting the other women,' she said. She was a family friend, she had delivered Irawati's other two children, as well as others in the family. Irawati had moaned even louder.

'It makes me feel better,' Irawati had told her. And then, when Gauri was born, strangely dark, far too small, her mother-in-law, Baya, had said, 'Call her Krishna, she is so blue, and she won't live too long anyway.'

Irawati, tired, relieved, and also defiant, had named her the opposite of Krishna: Gauri. And Gauri had lived, and thrived. She did not seem to mind when her mother went on research trips to the ends of the earth. Gauri complained to Irawati about Bhagirathi, who came to look after the children when her daughter was away, and tried to teach Gauri to do various things that would make her a bit more marriageable. Bhagirathi from her side complained to Irawati about Gauri running wild, and not wanting to be taught how to cook, or sew, or anything that might redeem her.

Irawati said to her mother, 'I don't know how to cook, and I did just fine, didn't I? You let me study what I wanted and marry who I wanted, so why worry about her now?' Irawati was happy, though, whenever Bhagirathi came to live with them. It gave Dinu some help and respite from looking after the children while she was away. Besides, Gauri complained that Dinu braided her hair too tight and made her look like a water buffalo with horns. She was happiest to be left to her own devices, running in the streets with the neighbourhood boys, and doing quite well at school. She went to the Ahilyabai Holkar High School along with her siblings, and she didn't get into much trouble there. There were complaints from neighbours about being pelted with pebbles from a catapult, and in all likelihood it was her, but it could have been any one of the neighbourhood children. But it was 1959 when they had started on this almost three-year sojourn, and Gauri had just turned seventeen, and she was no longer a child who climbed trees with the neighbourhood boys. They could not leave her behind. There was really no one they could have left her with anymore. Jai, the oldest of the three children, was married and living a few hours by car away from Pune, in Phaltan, Anand was in Germany, learning German before beginning his own PhD in biology in the city of Tübingen.

And so Gauri accompanied her parents to Berkeley, where

they could keep an eye on her, and she was signed up for classes at the university that would keep her out of trouble, or so they hoped. But Berkeley, California, in 1959 was about to tumble into The Sixties. And take all of America, and the world, with it. Gauri would not be left behind, no matter how much Irawati and Dinu might have wished otherwise.

~

There was a television in the house. The three of them watched the news together most evenings. A presidential election was imminent, and a certain young senator from Massachusetts, although he did not announce his candidacy till January of 1960, was travelling the length and breadth of the country, letting people become familiar with a name many had never heard. Dinner discussions at the Karve household were heated in spite of there being only the three of them most nights. Gauri was full of enthusiasm about Senator John F. Kennedy, and reported that many of her friends and fellow students were too. The fact that he was Catholic, to their surprise, was a big subject and a big issue for him politically. *Newsweek* magazine ran a cover story about it in June that year, Irawati brought a copy home, and they talked about it. Religion and politics were not uncommon subjects for discussion in the Karve household by any means. Surrounded by religious society—most of the population was religious in both thought and practice—in a country that had been split in two because of religion, and being in a family in which atheism was almost taken for granted, these discussions came up often. Usually they revolved around Hinduism, or the way Hinduism slid or scraped against the other religions in India. Irawati herself, brought up first in Burma and then in the other atheist

Paranjpye household, had her own views on the matter. She was not like Dinu, who was so very clear in his. For him, belief in anything that required belief was an intellectual weakness, and one which, far too often, and to the detriment of all society, was used as an excuse for terrible behaviours, big and small.

There was an incident in Pune involving a jasmine vine that Dinu had planted that grew over the perimeter fence of their house. He had tended it with great care and vigilance, and he enjoyed the fragrance and beauty of the white, precise flowers that bloomed abundantly all year. One day, very early in the morning, he was strolling in his blue striped white pyjamas and a sweater, admiring his jasmines and gerberas and the Chinese roses covering the slope from the house to the fence, when he saw an older gentleman in a dhoti and Nehru cap, a small wicker basket in hand. As Dinu watched, he hooked the vine with his walking stick and pulled it toward him, and then plucked the flowers and dropped them in his basket. Dinu was nothing less than incensed.

'Hey you thief,' he shouted, 'stop mauling my vine!'

The man stopped only for a moment and smiled serenely and said, 'Oh I'm not a thief, these are for my morning puja, don't worry,' and then reached out his cane again.

Dinu could not believe his ears. 'You are most definitely a thief,' he said to the man, 'go grow your own flowers for this puja, and leave mine alone!'

'But it's for God,' said the man, thoroughly confused.

'This nonsense may work with everyone else,' Dinu said. 'Not with me. These are my flowers, and they are not for your god.' He started menacingly toward the man, who finally understood, and, shaking his head and muttering about godless people coming back in other lives as various undesirable things, he hurried away. He made sure to walk past the jasmines and shake his head pointedly every time he saw Dinu outside. It was not just such things that irked Dinu. It was the proliferation of religiosity in every aspect of Indian life, big and small. He hated the smug and entitled behaviour of people who thought they had a sanction from god to do as they pleased.

Irawati admired him, his certainty, in thought and action. It was this same certainty with which he stood by her and behind her and for her, when she had embarked on her PhD in Berlin, in that case his certainty about her intellect. But she was not of the same thinking as her husband in this matter. To Irawati, as an anthropologist and also as a person, religion, particularly Hinduism, was so tied up in the philosophy and the history of the country, that she could not reduce it to just a belief in god. Hinduism was a loose set of beliefs without even a name, until, as she says in her *Hindu Society: An Interpretation*,[84] that the term 'Hindu' was coined by Muslims and gave a new consciousness of one-ness to people who were so designated. It was, according to her, a political act by those in power, in this case the Mughals. A differentiating, othering act, to designate those who were not Muslims. She also says that Hinduism itself coalesced into a religion in the face of opposition, in the face of confrontation with monotheistic religions. Although her views on this softened as she grew older and wiser, Irawati had written very sharp comments about her suspicion towards different monotheisms, be it religious or political, questioning the blind adoration of any one leader. In any case, Irawati considered herself a Hindu, and not only because she was *not* Christian, Muslim, Jewish, Shinto but because she drew deeply from the philosophies and histories that founded and were foundational principles within what is called Hinduism.

Irawati spoke of, and wrote about, religion and society in India over the two years that they were in California. There at Berkeley, at the Colloquium of South Asian Studies, she held a series of lectures on social, cultural, and historical aspects of the Hindu caste system. She took the chance to be in dialogue with several North American colleagues, like the Harvard-based anthropologist Clyde Kluckhohn. These were lectures and conversations that eventually culminated in her book, the year after she left California.

While she spent so much time thinking about and writing *Hindu Society* in California, themes like religion, politics and morals permeated her conversations in her daily life in the United States. The context of Kennedy's Catholicism in a largely Protestant country was more interesting to her than it was to Dinu, but they talked to each other about everything. Gauri, as with all their children, was always part of the conversations. The family was where their ability to construct thoughts and ideas into arguments, and the ability to present these confidently was nurtured and honed, guided by their mother and father. Irawati and Dinu created a setting that showed their children that they valued, sometimes above all else, this intellectual capacity.

'Today one of the boys asked me what it was like to live in such an *underdeveloped* country,' Gauri said as they ate the dinner she and Dinu had cooked together.

'And what did you tell them?'

'I asked them if it's so underdeveloped then how come both my parents have been invited to come all the way here and teach you.'

They all laughed, though they knew that was not really an answer. It was just a response to the inevitable and endless racism that came at her from all sides, about her accent, her clothes and hair, comments pointing to how exotic she was or how foreign, questions that didn't express any wish to know anything but were just more thinly veiled barbs, and ultimately displays of the asker's own ignorance. Gauri just wanted to shut people up. Irawati knew the feeling, she had encountered it too, through her life of travels to so many corners of the world. Sarcasm was a particular trait of the family, and extended family, one that outsiders often found jolting and even hurtful. But the racism was somehow worse here, at least to them, and particularly when delivered with self-righteous smugness that warranted the sorts of humorous and wickedly sarcastic responses that Gauri had learned as a member of her own family, her extended kin, and the Chitpavan community, and as a citizen of Pune—a city whose inhabitants are known for their unambiguous straightforwardness. She felt they all deserved it, and her parents did not discourage her.

Gauri did not stop at giving up wearing saris and the other Indian clothes she had brought with her. One day she went with Dinu to the barbershop where he had gone for his weekly trim, and got her hair cut off. She wore her jeans and sneakers all the time, and said that enough was enough with trying 'not to look Mexican.' People did not direct their anti-Mexican sentiments toward her when she played the part of the Oriental maiden, but she had had it with putting up with the anti-foreigner racism. She gave up trying to project something alien that she was not, to protect herself from being abused for the alien that she was. Irawati was sad for her, but also a little exhausted by her. This was her difficult child, the youngest child.

And just as she was beginning to wonder if they should have left her at home after all, it came out that Gauri now had a boyfriend.

Dinu and Irawati had decided to walk to the Greek Theatre together, they wanted to see it, and the views from there which they had been told were wonderful. They walked slowly, and stopped often because Irawati would feel a little breathless or tired. It was, in spite of those reasons, a pleasant way to get to a place. They saw things they otherwise missed, like the little wildflowers on the ground where they sat to catch a breath, or pretty pebbles that she put in his pants pocket. They saw a small animal that Irawati informed him was a mole, and that reminded them about the small droppings they had seen in the kitchen the last few days. They wondered what animal that might be. They decided to tell the landlady about it.

When they got to the theatre, there was a group of students in the front seats of the amphitheatre, and they seemed to be shouting and heckling a person on the stage. It looked like an impromptu rather than formal or large gathering, and definitely loud. They stopped there and watched for a while. It was Dinu who caught sight of his daughter first, and before he could tell her, Irawati saw her too. Gauri, pointing and clearly heckling the man on the stage, and a young man beside her, with hair cut so severely short and so pale blond that it looked like a halo around his head. He had his arm around Gauri's waist, possessively, naturally, as if they were used to it.

'Gandhari had given birth, not to a hundred sons, but a hundred sorrows,' she thought. She did not have a hundred sons, just this Gauri now to worry about. They walked back even slower than they had on the way there. They talked, because they talked about everything.

Irawati and Dinu believed deeply in independent thought, in freedom of thought and action, but now, they had come up against their limit. This was their own teenage daughter, asserting her independence of thought and action, just as her parents had brought her up to do. In spite of all their principles and beliefs in the liberty of their children, they were, after all, Indian parents, and they had, as Gauri herself put it years later, 'centuries of traditional mores dinned into their psyches,'[85] about the sexuality of women in general, and in particular, the importance of a woman's virginity. Their oldest child, Jai, was married to a man whose mother was an American Quaker from Pennsylvania. Anand was in love with, and determined to marry, Gudrun, in Germany. Now Gauri seemed to have lost that all important virtue to a young man with ice blue eyes and white-blond hair, and they wondered if she should marry him and be done with it. Gauri, though, had no such plan. There were tears and angry words, and Irawati despaired for her youngest child. She forgot, as all parents do. She forgot that she herself had broken all the big and small rules, had done and been things that were not accepted in the society of the time, and all those things had brought her where she was today: a respected and admired academic of great stature in India and in the world.

In spite of all the little and large tensions and troubles familial and outside, daily life went on, and in its way, the routine helped them all to cope. Irawati cooked, and Gauri helped. Dinu was happier to walk down to the grocery store and do the shopping. Irawati sent him off to buy rice one afternoon. Dinu came back triumphantly, with something that looked like unpolished rice. To Irawati's annoyance, which she freely expressed, it turned out to be orzo, an Italian wheat pasta shaped like large-grained rice.

'It says right on the package, Dinu, how could you think this is rice?'

'You thought so too, until you read the label,' Gauri said in her father's defence. She did seem to be on her father's side more often than Irawati's. It might have been the tension that began after the boyfriend debacle. But it caused Irawati anguish, and that did not help matters with her health.

Then something happened that improved their lives at home. The mysterious animal droppings in the kitchen started appearing again, and Dinu informed the landlady. She came by one Saturday morning to take a look.

'It's mouse droppings,' she said, and laughed. 'We'll see what we can do.'

On Sunday morning a man arrived carrying a box. When he opened it, a small calico cat jumped out and immediately began to wander around the house. This, apparently, was the landlady's solution.

'Her mother is a known mouser,' the man informed them, 'she's learned from the best.'

Irawati named the little cat Chitra, because she was tricoloured and patchy, and she became a most welcome new member of the family. As a bonus, the animal droppings disappeared. Chitra, as cats do, also improved everyone's mood and attitude to one another. She would sit on Irawati's lap in the evening, and when she ran her fingers through the soft fur and listened to the engine of her contentment, she felt content too, as if the ruffled fur of her feelings was being smoothed down.

Dinu brought the mail in one afternoon. He gave it to her on the sofa where she sat in the evenings after work, reading a magazine, papers or a novel. She had been told to take care of herself, and not doing work-related things after she returned from the university was one of the recommendations of the doctor and nurses, as well as of all the friends and family members who were worried about her health.

'There is a letter for you, Iru,' he said, 'and Gauri, two letters for you.'

Irawati looked at the letter. She recognised Appa's handwriting, it was more familiar to her than perhaps anyone else's. Dinu gave her the letter opener and she carefully opened the envelope. Her eyes welled up. 'He's really not in the best of health himself, and he went all the way to the building of the Bharat Sevak Samaj to ask what medicines Srinivasa Shastri was taking for his angina twenty-five years ago!' she said. 'But, has he forgotten that I am being looked after by the world's best doctors with the most advanced medical care—and that this medicine is probably obsolete by now,' she said, laughing through her tears.

~

In 1964, Irawati returned to San Francisco, this time at the invitation of Mills College. By this time, Gauri was married, to Avinash Deshpande, and had a child. Jai and her youngest baby daughter accompanied Irawati. They lived for half the year in Oakland. It was a pleasant time, they both liked everything about Northern California: the weather, the landscape, the people. California was always a place of political and creative energy. For Irawati this was a break from responsibilities at Deccan College, an opportunity to see old friends and make new ones, and to interact with her peers. This time was not fraught like the last, Irawati was not as tired or troubled by her health or her wild younger daughter.

On the way to America they had stopped in Germany, and visited, among others, Ria and Karl Seebass in Leipzig. They had always stayed in touch, but Irawati had never forgiven the older members of the family for their support of the Nazis. Most of the German people who were not persecuted and murdered were either Nazis or supported them, either actively or by consequence of their political inaction.

Writing about the German philosopher Heidegger,[86] his musings about being and not being, Irawati says that once a thing is in hand, taking that thing to its very absolute limit, never letting it go, is a German virtue. Like steamrollers, crushing stone into gravel, compacting it. The truth, she says, is always before you. It is not hidden, nor does it need to be excavated. The only reason you cannot see it, is that you are not ready to see it. Like Munch's scream, like the scream of the suicidal woman in Camus' novel, the silence of so many of her German friends and colleagues, the silence of an entire people was a truth she could not, and did not, turn away from.

Part Four

15

Weeping Plateau

Late in 1945, Kanyakumari: Irawati and Dinkar stood at the end of the world, at the confluence of the Indian Ocean, the Arabian Sea, the Bay of Bengal—where the names we give the water lose their meaning, where they were unable to imagine that land beyond that place was even a possibility. Irawati wondered how people in a distant past might have pushed boats into that seemingly endless ocean, and found out that there were, in fact, lands beyond this watery universe. In all her writing, it is so clear how much she was of the world, and really in the world. She put herself in the thoughts and imaginations of other humans who might have stood where she stood, gone where she had not. Irawati thought about how close Lanka looks on a map and how far it must actually be: she couldn't see it from where they stood. And there, at that calm sea level flatness, the ripples spreading out as far as their eyes could see, they talked about the great mountain range across all the land of India, and Irawati said to Dinu, 'We must travel to the Himalayas one day, you and I.'

It was many years before they managed to synchronise their vacations, have Bhagirathi come and take care of the children and the house, find reasonably priced tickets, and finally leave Pune for the ancient pilgrimage route of Badri-Kedar. First they had to travel north, and the subcontinent was sweltering in the high months of summer. The train journey felt unending because of the relentless heat. The train rattled through the heated ranges of the Sahyadris, the Satpudas and the Vindhyas. Irawati saw heat mirages during the day on the Gangetic plains, and in the pitch darkness of night, she felt as if she and her fellow travellers were all cakes and biscuits cooking in a constantly vibrating oven. Only when the train left the southern plains did the temperatures drop, and the view outside told them they were in Himalayan territory, approaching Dehradun. This old town set among four to five thousand foot high peaks with its red-roofed houses and views was delightful to Irawati, but the travel beyond that left memories of heat and dust, beggars and slimy travel agents, and corrupt travel companies. In spite of all this, she always felt that this pilgrimage, if at all possible, was worth doing at least once in a lifetime.

The normal way to go on this pilgrimage was to find an agent, and there were many of these. This man would be responsible for arranging transportation—which included everything from bus tickets to horses or mules, as well as luggage carriers, a cook, a dogsbody, someone who could show them where to stay at night and so on. Irawati has written a detailed and lengthy essay about this pilgrimage. She records all her observations about the flora—that clematis flowers are three times the size of the ones in Dinu's garden, that mountain violets do not have a fragrance, and that bay leaves in South India are more fragrant than those in the Himalayas. She pressed never before seen flowers into a diary to be identified later as rhododendrons by a botanist in Dehradun on their return journey. She talks about the pilgrims being so different from each other and showing the diversity of the land in their languages, their food and dress, the way they looked and spoke and interacted with one another. There is an instance where she feels great pleasure when she sees a group of widows talking and laughing together with other women, because in Maharashtra, where a widow is a creature so wretched, a 'living corpse', such a sight is an impossibility. There are words she hears people pronounce that are said differently in Maharashtra, and she observed how kinship terms varied depending on where people came from.

Throughout this trip Irawati was also a photographer, using sometimes black and white, and sometimes colour film in the camera she had received as a gift in Berlin from the physicist Lise Meitner, a dear friend she never got to see again. Irawati's son-in-law, Avinash, Gauri's first husband, had asked her where she had got that beautiful camera, and when she replied, 'Lise Meitner', she was taken aback when he said he knew of her. That Avinash, an electrical engineer by training, knew of Meitner and reacted with amazement, was a particular pleasure for Irawati. No one outside Meitner's fields had heard of her, even in Irawati's large academic circle. Though she had gone on to great heights, like the women of her time, Meitner didn't receive as much recognition as she deserved. The Nobel Prize, for one, was never given to her, though she had been nominated nineteen times for chemistry, and thirty times for physics.

With her Leica, Irawati photographed Kamet peak in early morning moonlight, and said about the nature of photographs and memory that one appreciates a photograph only after memory has faded. To her, though places exist in the world that look better in photographs than actuality, the Himalayas are not one of these places: the unframeable beauty of that mountainous scenery could not be captured in a single photo.

Even though they were on a pilgrimage to the country's most sacred places, Irawati and Dinu did not perform the religious rituals that most people made the rather difficult journey to these pilgrimage sites to do. But when they were at the main temple at Kedar, their guide who had been with them all the way asked Irawati, 'With what intention did you come? With what desire?' All pilgrims came with a wish they wanted fulfilled, they came to ask a favour from the high gods of these sacred mountains, so it was quite normal to ask this question of a pilgrim. Irawati did not answer him. Looking at the scene before her she thought:

> *Intention? Desire? Never, I had none. I had no mind left. The blue sky above, did that have desires? Did the black rocks have some intention? Were those ranges and ranges of mountains standing there for a reason? I was one of them, that blue sky, those slopes, those mountains. I was the infinite sentience and the sky.*[87]

Although Irawati did not make the Himalayan pilgrimage with a traditional Hindu bent of mind, she did choose that particular journey rather than any other. It took money and time and effort to make it possible, and she could have chosen some other spot for a vacation or gone to see the Himalayas on a trek or as a tourist. She went as a pilgrim, along with other Hindu pilgrims. She felt the pull of that aspect of those places they visited, and she wrote of those feelings. She said that she saw people from all corners of the country—people who did not dress alike or speak the same language, or even worship the same gods. What they did have in common, she says, was the reverence for these sacred places. This is what had brought these diverse people on this pilgrimage, and this is what they had in common—she calls this, too, Hindu culture. In 1947, in the heat of India's independence and the agony of Partition, Irawati had written that this Hindu culture was what made this country an entity, and that it was—apart from all the politics around it—what fixed the borders as this country called India.[88] It is difficult to know how Dinu approached these views of hers, or if he was influential in her evolving views on national unity and the existence of non-Hindu Indians that is seen later in her writings. Perhaps it was because she reflected on the trauma of Partition, and the absurdity of the politics of communal identity that led to violence, exclusion, and bigotry that she argued, very explicitly, that India could be home to everyone who called themselves Indian, independent of their religion or language. She saw what her own family had become, and liked it. And perhaps she foresaw what it would become: a family of atheists, Quakers, Muslims, Sikhs, Catholics and Protestants, Marxists, people who were not from the same state, country, or even continent as herself let alone the same caste, her grandchildren and great-grandchildren not recognisable as any 'race' but the human race, in its many shades and creeds. In a speech in the 1960s she said:

> *Race, religion, caste all lead to mutual prejudice which in the modern setting can be translated into race-jingoism but I emphasise again: we [Indians] are all thorough mongrels who have been thrown together and must learn to lessen our prejudices and live together.*[89]

Even back in the 1940s, though, she wrote that monotheism, like monoculture, would create a listless, monotonous forest of indistinctive individuals. But it wasn't the existence of one-

God-only religions per se that troubled her, it was the threat to the diversity of beliefs. Religious and political supremacists terrified and angered her. She likened the extreme parties and ideologies to each other, and writes that there is no difference between those who blindly followed a single leader as if that leader were an almighty god. Whether that leader was Mohammad, Gandhi, Stalin, or the RSS chief and Hindu supremacist Golwalkar,[90] she writes, their followers are frightening illustrations of an unbending monotheism. She worried that humanity was being poisoned by this thinking that everyone must belong to one of these sects, and no one is allowed, under threat of annihilation, to speak against the apostles. Every party and every religion has this kind of extreme thinking, she says, just replace 'Muhammad Rasulillah' with 'Gandhi Rasulillah', 'Stalin Rasulillah' and 'Golwalkar Rasulillah'.[91]

While Irawati's angry views on fanatic 'monotheisms' (and her equating these very different political and religious leaders) might sound biased according to her own polytheistic Hindu belief, and possibly biased against Islam, she made sure to make it clear some years later that a person of any faith or non-faith, Muslims or Christians, can call India their home. She believed that India does not have to aspire to be a Hindu society. She said:

> *Our history shows in every century new people have come and made India their home...It is a fascinating subject for study to try to find out what we are—Indians as a whole, but it is entirely wrong to imagine ancestries and base claims on territories as somehow one's own. All those who are in India today, who feel it is their homeland are Indians...The society we want to build*

> *is not a Hindu society or a Hindi society but a multicultural, multilingual society which has knowledge of one another's culture and has decided to live and work together in comradeship.*[92]

Irawati got to see first-hand what political monotheism and religious fanaticism combined could look like. At some point early in her career she worked as an assistant to a magistrate and was responsible for adjudicating cases involving juvenile offenders. She felt great distress about the many young men who were brought before her for arson. She had seen the buildings they had burned down, she saw them as symbols of a poisoned generation. One of the youths brought before her in court told her that he would be willing to kill anyone if his leader asked him to. She holds the leaders and the philosophy of these 'monotheistic cults' responsible, saying, in palpable anguish:

> *It takes thousands of years to achieve humanitarian values, and one generation for them to come to dust.*[93]

~

Irawati lived, thought about, and carried within her the ancient philosophies of the Mahabharata, the Vedas, the Puranas, the ideas of dharma, karma, birth and rebirth, advaita and Brahman. But she also looked dispassionately, critically, and, again, with her anthropologist's mind at the multifaceted religiosity and philosophy of what is now called Hinduism. At the same time that she participated in Hindu rituals, she was fully aware of its shortcomings, and, mainly, its existence as a human-made structure—concepts, gods, and all. And yet, she would return to and express those feelings in her writings, of oneness with the limitless, of the eternity of existence. She knew about the power of spirituality to guide one through difficult times and questionings, its power as a well of meaning from which to fulfil and replenish a trivial life.

In 1954, of her and Dinu's Himalayan journey she wrote,

> *We had spent the last twenty days and nights in each other's company, in the Himalayas, in the home of the gods. For a moment at least, I had experienced infinity there, on the summit of Tunganath. Isn't this golden moment enough to light up my life?*[94]

She also had misgivings about the political direction of the country in a way that seems prescient. About the same diversity she so admires about India she says:

> *Language, ethnicity, dress styles, are not obstacles to this sense of oneness. Instead, these differences, this diversity itself is the core of our unity. It seems today that politicians are afraid of difference and diversity. There is a fight to centralise rule, and I think this has not to do with cultural issues, but with the consolidation of power to the centre.*[95]

This same Hindu culture that she sees defining India's borders for thousands of years also causes her anguish. In the concluding paragraphs of *Yuganta*, comparing today's Indians—today's Hindus—with those in the Mahabharata, Irawati's question, asked sixty years ago, sounds as if she flung it at us today:

> *How did we accept the dreamy escapism of 'bhakti' and blind hero worship after having faced and thought undauntingly of the hard realities of life? How did the people who used to eat all meats including beef begin*

> *to find salvation in ritually drinking the urine and eating the dung of the cow, and calling this quadruped their mother?*

Irawati was a Hindu of the Mahabharata: one who followed her dreams and ambitions, and who ate beef, not just because it was a dire necessity but because she didn't see it as the major sin of Hinduism—she was against the 'beef ban' even then.[96] She says she cannot answer her own question, and only asks it to provoke thought. But there is an answer to be found in her next lines.

> *I am indeed fortunate that I can read today a story called 'Jaya', which was sung three thousand years ago, and discover myself in it.*

Perhaps she means that if an Irawati can find herself in 'Jaya'—the original story upon which the Mahabharata was built—then all Indians can.

~

The Bhima river becomes a crescent as it curves at the town of Pandharpur, so there the river has the sweet name of Chandrabhaga. In Pandharpur lives Vithoba. He has stood on a brick in the temple since before memory. Vithoba was there before Irawati found her way to him, and there he still stands, and always will, though Irawati will never again visit him. In her essay 'Boyfriend?' Irawati talks about her many visits to see this god, and she says he waits for her, and when she goes to him, he says to her, 'So. You have remembered me.' Irawati says he implies that something in her life made her remember Vithoba, something that is lacking. When Irawati travelled to Pandharpur it was in a car, with the family driver, and perhaps one of her daughters, or friends. The road took her through Phaltan, where Jai lived, and she stopped there and visited with her, her three granddaughters and her son-in-law. She went when the weather was clear, when the roads would not be inundated by flash floods, when she felt well enough for a road trip, and when Dinu would not be inconvenienced if she took their car and driver. She was no Meera or Bahinabai or Sakhu—the women saints of Maharashtra and Rajasthan, who left their homes and husbands, because they wanted nothing but to be with their divine lords. There are men in Maharashtra too, who see the god Vitthal[97] as their lover and, because He must always be the superior, they assume the female role in their relationship with him, and wear black beads at their throats and wrists.

The essay about Vithoba begins with a question Irawati's son-in-law asked on her return from one of her trips to Pandharpur: 'Well, did you see your boyfriend?'

Irawati, reflecting on her relationship with Vithoba, concludes that indeed the god is not her boyfriend, because she sees herself as being at a great distance from him—'unfortunately.' She talks of this god as if he were real, and exists, and knows of her existence, of her troubles in her life.

Before these convenient (if not luxurious) car trips, when Irawati was younger and healthier, when she and Vithoba saw each other for the very first time, she had walked fifteen days to get to Pandharpur.

Irawati did not consider her short essays part of her scientific work, they were published in magazines and in book collections, and were written for a Marathi-speaking readership. Only a few have been translated into English. One of these essay collections was *Yuganta*,[98] which, in 1968, won her the Sahitya Akademi Award, India's most acclaimed literature prize, and which inspired a tradition of Marxist, feminist, and Dalit interpretations of the Mahabharata. Another of her essays is 'Watchaal' (On the Road), which details, as a pilgrim and as an observer, her long walk to meet, for the first time, this Vithoba, who was waiting for her at Pandharpur. Irawati did not come from a family who belonged to the cult of Vithoba, and nor, of course, did the atheist Karves and Paranjpyes, so she had never been to Pandharpur. It is a mystery as to why she became enamoured of Vithoba, why he should sit so deeply in her heart and mind, so much so that she was willing to join the annual pilgrimage and walk all the way from Pune to Pandharpur. The way she wrote about Vithoba, and the way she talked about him, this was clearly not a journey undertaken for fieldwork alone, or at all. Nor did she stop with the one visit, she went to Pandharpur many times throughout her life. Irawati said to her family and to her militantly atheist husband that her practice of religion was cultural. But this does not explain why she went to Pandharpur again and again through her life, to see this stone statue in a hot and dusty Maharashtrian town, to lay her head upon those stone feet and speak of him as a comfort in times of trouble, just as any other devotee of any other god would do.

The essay 'On the Road' is full of detail about the walk. The heat and clouds, the villages and towns they passed through on their days-long march, the meals they ate, the bullocks and dogs, and, her fellow pilgrims—are all written about, lovingly, it can be said. And then there is Vithoba himself. Irawati was fascinated by the relationship individual pilgrims have with their god. A theme comes up again and again as she talks to men and women. A woman in the depths of sorrow tells Irawati that her only son, a young man in his twenties, had died. Another woman talks of her great sorrow that she never had any children and how empty her life and her house are. A man who has lost his wife and children in an epidemic says to Irawati, 'You know, Vitthal is a very hard god. If your heart gets entangled in something, he tears it out.' All these people acknowledge that this same Vithoba, to whom they are now walking, having left their towns and villages and families and lives to go see, is the one who creates their sorrows, and also the one to whom they turn for solace when he does. Irawati asks Vithoba, 'Why do you let it [the heart] get entangled in the first place? And why then do you tear it out? What greatness do you get from this?' and then, surprised at herself, thinks again.

> *Oh but I was out of my mind! The agony of the old woman made me forget the world for a moment. Who brings whom to his feet? It's all a play of the human mind. First it creates a god with qualities out of a completely indifferent, formless and attributeless principle, then makes him the author of everything that happens, makes him the Lord of the universe, and then says, 'We can only have what he does not take.'*[99]

She demonstrates here that since gods create the concepts of sorrow or joy that affect human life, they are before, and therefore immune, to such things, but also, in an ouroboros logic, that the human mind creates these gods.

Irawati, at the end of the journey, feels anguish as they approach Pandharpur. These people, who have been her companions on the road, with whom she has shared the sorrows and joys of her life, and who in turn have opened their hearts to her, will soon be parted from her. She knows, as they do, that they will never, in this life, see each other again. As they approach the final steps of the plateau, her own eyes, and those of every person around her, are streaming. In her sadness, she looks around, for The One who has walked with them. She sees him, his back to her, walking away in the other direction. Her words, at the end of that essay, speak to every heart, be they atheist or devotee of Vithoba.

> *'Why, Dark One, are You leaving too? Are You not coming to Pandharpur?' He smiled and shook his head. 'Where are You off to?' Without a word, He merely waved His arm and began to walk fast. The black ploughed fields and the sky full of heavy black clouds soon engulfed that delicate dark figure with the blanket on His shoulder. And I stepped inside the gates of Pandharpur with streaming eyes, weary legs, and a heavy heart.*[100]

Irawati's Marathi essays reveal sides of her that are not always visible in her English and academic work. These are personal works, and she wrote them so that she could speak about her ways of thinking and looking at the world—especially those that were not academic. Taken together with her scholarly work, they reveal the multitudes that she contained: she is that anthropologist, that intellectual and distanced observer, aware that we make these Khandobas and Vithobas, perhaps not in our image but to give us solace and succour, so we can lay the blames of our existence at their feet. And, standing on the final stretch of ground that would take her to Pandharpur, the place of parting the pilgrims called the weeping plateau, she shows us, whether she knows it or not, that she herself belongs to the cult of Vithoba.

~

Jai translated those few of Irawati's essays that are available to English readers. In one of these,[101] it is possibly Jai herself in a conversation with her mother as they walk along a street in Pune where a new housing complex is coming up. A temple has been constructed, and the person accompanying Irawati is irritated about yet another temple in a city that already has far too many. Irawati then translates an old Tamil proverb for her companion—'One should not have a house in a town without a temple.' Irawati decides, she says somewhat mischievously, to use the opportunity to show off her learning then—unaware that being able to quote an ancient Tamil proverb has already done that—and proceeds to explain patiently why she agrees with this old proverb. Her knowledge also extends to the city that was her home much of her life: Pune. The temple that started the discussion on that walk is a Maruti temple, and she says there are various Maruti temples in the different quarters of Pune. The Bhangya Maruti (Hashish Maruti), Pasodya Maruti (Maruti of the quilts), and the sex workers' quarter is where Chinnal Maruti—'the whoring Maruti'—has his own temple. She says,

> *A temple gives form to the formless. It is where that which has no beginning is installed, and on occasion that which has no end is destroyed.*[102]

In today's India, where the eye will find no temple free horizon, where larger and larger Ganesh and Saibaba statues are remaking the land into a Hinduscape, where the Pandharpur pilgrimage is now a commercially sponsored event that draws people in the hundreds of thousands, Irawati might have been at least a little uncomfortable. Perhaps she would be saddened, angered even, by the obsession with a single animal, and the making of the cow as well as various historical figures into mascots for a manufactured religion that bears no likeness to the ancient teachings she was so familiar with. Perhaps she had foreseen all of this. Perhaps she forewarned us, in her way, of what was to come, when she wrote about the Dark One turning away from the gates of Pandharpur. Hers is a powerful, poignant, and even pessimistic message after all, of a god abandoning those most in need of him: the God Vithoba, walking away from the pilgrims who had gathered there for a glimpse of him, without a word, she says, without a backward glance, into the gathering storm.

16

Brahman

The Deccan Traps are some of the most interesting geological regions in the world. The Yucatan meteor which caused the extinction of dinosaurs triggered massive volcanic eruptions on the opposite side of planet Earth, more massive than any before or since. One result of this cataclysmic incident is the Sahyadri Mountains, and the sweet little hill station of Mahabaleshwar. A few hours' drive up the Western Ghats from Pune, this town, sitting in the basalt hills that were thrust fourteen hundred metres up from sea level by those ancient volcanoes, was a favourite of Irawati's. She would go there to escape the unbearable searing dry heat of Pune's summers, with Dinu, the children when they were younger, and with grandchildren later in her life.

In the late 1950s, Irawati and Dinu had moved into the house they would live in for the rest of their lives, in Gultekdi, on the outskirts of Pune. This was a larger and cooler house than the one at Law College Road, but it was still Pune, and summers were still best escaped, and Mahabaleshwar, with its cool nights and pleasant days, was irresistible. They would stay at the Hotel Girivihar whenever possible, a place where she was known and welcomed as a valued guest. Irawati loved the

Montane forests of the Mahabaleshwar plateaus—subtropical canopies that were not very tall and felt close overhead making her introspective forest walks intimate and cool. Waking up to the predictable morning call of the koel, listening to the nonchalant unmelodic whistling of the Malabar thrush in the afternoon, the bold rhesus monkeys that gathered around their yard, the more cautious langurs that watched her with warm brown eyes in seamed black leather faces, the thrill of spotting a giant red squirrel on a high branch if she was very quiet—all this was Mahabaleshwar. If she saw the little white paradise flycatcher with his long tail feathers floating behind him, she considered herself very lucky indeed. The sunsets from various lookout points illuminating the folds upon folds of the stone walls of the hills were quietly spectacular. They brought on a kind of reverence within her, a feeling of oneness with the world—even the universe—and everything in it.

Irawati's own spiritual and philosophical ideas arose from the ancient Sanskrit texts that she had read and thought about all her life: the Upanishads, the Vedas. She was also well versed in other religions, of India and the world. But her own heart and mind, if those were separate things, belonged to the philosophy of ancient India. Irawati revelled in that feeling of belonging to the world. She writes in her essay 'All This is You' about this feeling, an expanding sensation that flooded her as she sat on a hill at the end of the day and watched the orange sky and the clouds and the mountains. The feeling of being one with the sunset, with her little granddaughter, even with the dog who came to her with his joyfully wagging tail. They all shared the same breath of life that made them so alive. She belonged to the same substance as they did, the substance of the universe: they all were of the One. There is an idyllic sinking into the beauty of this Oneness that would last but a few more days.

Back home in Pune, on the morning of April 12, 1961, Irawati, still in the glow of her universal beinghood, picks up the newspaper. The headline reads:

Eichmann Faces Trial on Charges of Genocide.

On April 11, 1961, the day before that headline appeared in the Indian press, the Nazi Adolf Eichmann's trial had begun in Jerusalem, after being captured some months earlier by Mossad agents in Argentina. Small and large, regional and national newspapers all over the world covered the trial.[103] That morning when Irawati read those words, her thoughts, her well-being, her very worldview took a strange turn. In one of her most personal essays Irawati opens herself to her reader and comes as close as she ever has to a revelation of regret. How would she reconcile her feelings of Oneness with the world, if the world was also made of banal evil? If in fact she believed that she was the sunset and the smile of her granddaughter and the wag of the puppy's tail, then, she thought, she must also be made of the same substance as Eichmann and all the Nazis—the people who had murdered millions of people, including people she knew.

> *I had known of course that the Nazis had tortured and killed millions of innocent men, women, children. But I still could not bear to read this account of the atrocities committed by one single man. I thought of my friends who had lost their lives in this holocaust, and of other friends who had escaped and been saved but whose lives were ruined, meaningless. Hatred swelled up in me, hatred against their murderers. And then came the thought: 'They are also you.' I felt as though I had received an electric shock. No, no. Never. How*

> *can those for whom I feel nothing but loathing and contempt be I? It is impossible. I brushed away this revolting cockroach that was trying to cling to me. My poor mind was silenced.*[104]

The effect of this conclusion, the logical next step to her thought process, is clear in her words. 'Shock', 'revolt', and 'disgust'. But she has not shied away from her conclusion, nor hidden it away in the recesses of her own mind. She surrendered to this brutal process of confrontation with the evil in the world and in herself. Eichmann's actions were responsible for an immeasurable scale of suffering and death. But if Eichmann was an ordinary man who was just obeying orders from above, as was consistently argued in his defence in the trial, could every ordinary person succumb to such evil? If criminal behaviour wasn't considered a genetic or racial trait anymore—as European racial theorists had believed in the past—can't anyone, independent of their biological makeup, turn to crime and violence? Yes. So, does each of us carry the seeds of evil and hate?

And such horrible violence did not just happen in Germany or Europe. Irawati had also seen it close to home, she thought, so she had to bring her confrontation back to home, back to herself. She might have asked: had her German colleagues, maybe even her *Doktorvater*, Eugen Fischer, expected the genocide that unfolded around them, and if they did, what could they have done to stop it? Did they even try to? And if her colleagues in Berlin had not foreseen the deep political implications of the racist and eugenicist knowledge they had put out into the world, what was her responsibility as a scientist and public intellectual in the troubles in her own home country? Hadn't she also shown indifference to the brutality of India's independence process against particular people and communities? Such questioning cast a shadow of doubt and humility on her. She asks, in her conversation with herself:

> *What effort have you made to destroy those seeds of hate? Haven't you lived in this same society by following the policy of saving your own skin? Then what is the point of saying that you share none of the responsibility for the crime in the world, in your own society? All of it is you.*[105]

In these lines, Irawati comes to terms with the acceptance of collective responsibility, if not guilt. One might be tempted to conclude that it is a justification, a turning away from responsibility. But she is clear in her essay that whether or not every person bears responsibility for every action, she holds herself to a standard that she admits having failed. This confession does not allow Irawati to set herself free (as Christian-Judaic confession would have done), it in fact draws her further into the philosophy of the self as non-dual, as material that only yearns, if that is possible, to return to a state that is undivided, and unseparated from the Whole. *Tat tvam asi*, she says: all that is you, and you are all that. She attempts as a separate being to extend the feeling of oneness, so easy to feel with what is perceived as 'good' or 'innocent' or 'beautiful', to everything: even that which is perceived as 'evil' or 'ugly' by the present being that she is.

~

On Eugen Fischer's eightieth birthday, prominent people from his life were invited to write a few lines of their impressions and memories of the man. These letters were to be presented to the retired anthropology professor as part of the celebrations. As one of his well-known students, Irawati was among the people who was asked to contribute. Her letter is an exercise in tact bordering on vagueness at first glance, and yet containing very personal experiences with her German *Doktorvater* from decades before. She wrote:

> *Which day to remember of the many memorable ones? I remember the day I went to him with a broken arm, lonely, not knowing what to do. He was, as usual, kind and gave work which could be done with one arm and which could keep me busy and happy in a vast unknown city…I also remember the day when I sat facing a window with trees bare of leaves, crying without being conscious of it. He came into the laboratory and putting his hands on my shoulder said but two sentences: 'The leaves will be back soon. The winter is over.' How did he know what was in my mind? He was scientific in his teaching, exacting but kind as a guide and always had a deep humanity. He and I belong to different religions, but I think he felt with me that all humanity, black and white, tall and short, was the manifestation and incarnation of the One Absolute. Thanks to his teaching as an anthropologist, this ancient teaching of the Hindus was manifested to me in a new light.*[106]

The Nazis came to power in Germany just a few years after Irawati left Berlin, and Eugen Fischer developed a close political and ideological involvement with the party, which took him further in his career. Whether he wanted or not, Fischer's racial anthropology and eugenics gave leverage to many of the political applications of this knowledge by the

Nazis, from laws aimed at racial purity to the genocide of millions of people who were deemed racially and genetically inferior and unfit, from Jews to Sinti and Roma, homosexuals, and people with disabilities. In the process of de-Nazification following the end of World War II, Fischer, like all his fellow researchers in Berlin (except one, his student and successor in the KWI-A direction, Wolfgang Abel, who was forced to retire and dedicate himself to painting landscapes), was never convicted. However, Fischer was to some extent scientifically, and surely historically, ostracised: his plans to reopen the KWI-A never succeeded, and anthropology and other sciences would slowly but steadily distance from that eugenicist thinking that thrived among the Nazis. Scientists continue to make efforts to tackle the complicated legacy of racial and racist thinking. From today's viewpoint and echoing some of his critics at that time (like German anthropologist Franz Boas who was exiled in the US), Fischer's racial anthropology is undoubtedly associated with the scientific racism that led to dehumanisation and genocide.

Irawati never met her *Doktorvater* again, and, like anyone else, she could never know what was in his mind, or how much he approved or disapproved of what had happened in Germany. Germany had a bitter-sweet place in her memories: she remembered her time in Berlin with some fondness, and rejoiced when her memory refreshed that feeling of something electric in the 1920s Berliner air, even though she often felt lonely—but she also felt the pain for the friends who suffered because of the Nazi persecution and war, and she had a hard time reconciling with those German colleagues and friends who had been indifferent or ambiguous to what had happened.

When Jai and Irawati travelled through Germany on their

way to America in 1964 and were to visit the Seebass family in Leipzig, the family Dinu and then Irawati had become so close with, Jai remembers her mother saying that some of the family had openly supported Hitler. When Jai asked Irawati if she would now confront them, Irawati replied in the negative: it was too long ago, she said, and she did not want to bring it up. She was grateful for what that family had done for her, and she did not believe it would change anything. Perhaps the choice between confrontation and rejection was too painful, and, as she also said to Jai—she would never see these people again. This may even have been a statement of intent, in which case she did make a choice.

Among their albums Irawati and Dinu kept a few photographs of Eugen Fischer: a tiny black and white portrait with Dinu's firm handwriting below it 'Iru's teacher Professor Fischer', Eugen Fischer in a white suit sitting with students under a tree, an indistinct profile at a window. In one photo, faded and cracked now, is a family gathered in a garden, perhaps just for the photograph. In the back row stands a young man in a black uniform with a black armband on his sleeve, black swastika clearly visible, and two young women in striped and floral dresses. In the front row is an older couple: a lady in a floral dress with a white lace collar, and a man in a black suit, an eagle and swastika pin faintly visible on his lapel. The man is Professor Eugen Fischer. There is no writing on the photograph to indicate who these people are, but it is probable that it is the Fischer family. The young Nazi soldier is the only one not smiling, almost sad, almost grim. There is also a dramatic black and white portrait signed on the rear with Fischer's best wishes to Irawati, much like a rock star or actor would send to his fans.

These photographs were most likely sent to Irawati after 1933, when she had left Berlin.

Irawati's birthday letter to the old Fischer praises what she wanted to remember from him: his deep sense of humanity. Someone who comforted her when she felt sad and cried. Perhaps, the story of the letter was her attempt to recuperate the human in him, someone who would be known as a Nazi scientist, but nevertheless human. It would have been too easy, too self-defensive and complacent, to think that Fischer and those who took part in Nazi crimes were inhuman, monsters even. But seeing the humanity in them—because they too are, of course, human—opens up a more self-challenging but insightful reflection: all of us humans carry the same potential, to love and to hate, to indifference and compassion, to good and evil. In the case of Eugen Fischer, so much else came with being human—being racist, being weak, being prone to hate and being a Nazi. In these reflections, Irawati learned the most difficult of lessons from Hindu philosophy: all *that* is you, too.

~

'When will you make kheer again?' Gauri asked her mother on day, as she ate the last of it.

'On your fifth birthday, Gauri. A year from today,' Irawati said. Gauri thought carefully before replying. 'So next Tuesday?' she said, to the amusement of Jai, Anand and Irawati.

Irawati recounts this story in her essay, 'Dikkal'[107] (Troubles). But Irawati didn't dismiss Gauri's perception of time. Time was a sensation, a feeling, desires, hopes. Experiences. Irawati's graduation was the same year as her little brother Sadashiv's munj ceremony, when her mother had a brand new sari. She could see them in her mind's eye, Sadashiv sitting on his mother's lap, the colours, the smells of that time and place. That year that Jai fell down the stairs. That year of the earthquake. Dinu was frustrated by this 'unscientific' way of thinking.

'Can't you just say the such and such day of April, the year such and such?' he would say, 'It is clear and precise.'

Irawati didn't agree. The days and years of her life were not numbers on a calendar, and certainly not points tied to the birth of Christ, a date which itself was suspect. She had never thought that these dates were not useful when it involved human history. But an individual understood time in other ways. There were minutes that for her had stretched out interminably because of grief, or fear, or pain. And there were entire years that were gone in a flash.

On the morning of August 11, 1970, Dinu had awoken early, as he always did, to walk in the garden of the house at Gultekdi. The house was built with red stone from Mahabaleshwar, with a sweeping enclosed balcony that he and particularly Irawati spent a lot of time in. She loved the big view of the bare hills surrounding Pune, with no other house or building in sight except for the nunnery on one side, halfway up a small hill. The red house had been a place of gatherings, of grandchildren and family—brothers and brothers-in-law, sons and sons-in-law, cousins, uncles, friends, colleagues, and visitors from all over the world. The walls were lined with shelves and full of books—John Steinbeck and Alistair Maclean and Jane Austen sat with volumes of Greek myths and legends and of course the Mahabharata in many languages and editions. Dinu had grown jasmines in the garden of this house too, and flowering pink gliricidia and purple jacaranda. The children had not grown up in this house, and even Irawati's mother had never visited them there. But they had been happy in this house.

That morning, after his walk, Dinu read his newspaper while he had his tea. He wondered why Irawati was not yet down for her breakfast. He went up the stairs to wake her, and he could not.

Irawati had taken her last breath during that night. Her heart, which had struggled for almost a decade, had finally stopped. She would never again have breakfast with him, or read to him from the morning paper, or walk in the shadow of the Himalayas, or the shade of their own trees. And it wouldn't be the date that he would remember, it was the moment of knowledge that his life was forever changed. A moment that would be with him to the end of his own time.

When the enormity of his loss settled into his heart, he said to Gauri, 'What will I do now?'

Indeed there were many many people who felt that way when they heard the news of Irawati's passing. Jai and Anand and Gauri, and her sons and daughters-in-law, her granddaughters and nephews and nieces and friends and colleagues and students, people who worked with and for her, in the country and in the world.

Many who were not even born when she lived, and who would never meet her, were touched by her life and work.

Dinu lived a decade without his Iru. He was never the same after she was gone, but his children and grandchildren, and all his friends, family and colleagues were grateful to have had him in their lives. He was, even in his final hours, the same deeply principled, quiet, logical man he had been all his life. He did not show fear or worry. The words of C.P. Cavafy in his poem when Mark Antony leaves Alexandria describe Dinu's leaving from the world he had known:

As one long prepared, and graced with courage,
As one for you who proved worthy of this kind of city[.][108]

Dinu died in his room in the house he had built with Irawati, with Gauri by his side, on July 5, 1980.

'If every animal can go to its death without a god,' he said to her, 'then so can I.' Gauri said of her beloved father, that Dinu had something that we all could aspire to: amazing grace.

~

Irawati writes in one of her books that,

> *Above all this phenomenal world, including it, permeating it and transcending it, is the absolute being called Brahman (a neuter noun). This is thought of as a spiritual reality and in that context is called paramatman (the ultimate soul) as opposed to the individual atman (soul), which lives in the world of phenomena. The individual soul must wander through space and time, through many births, round and round in the great circle of phenomena (samsara-chakra, or sometimes called simply samsara) until it finds final release by the knowledge of its oneness with the Absolute Soul.*
>
> *The theory then is as follows. The ultimate reality is Brahman. This is realised by a seeker in three stages which are given in three sentences in the Upanishads. The sentences are: 'I am Brahman', 'You are Brahman', 'Indeed, all is Brahman.'*
>
> *This means that everything that is, is Brahman. Does it mean that Brahman is merely another word for the totality of the phenomenal world? No, definitely not. The phenomenal world is bounded by time and space. Everything in it has a beginning and an end and is at*

> *a particular place. It has also qualities like red, white, smooth, rough, cruel, kind, good or bad. The Brahman is infinite, eternal and above all qualities, but at the same time all the phenomenal world is its manifestation. The analogy given to illustrate this point is: 'A ripple on the ocean is ocean, but does not exhaust the ocean.'*
>
> *This conception leads to the thought that the world of human values—the most dearly held of human possessions—has no absolute reality and that everything being a manifestation of Brahman has a right to exist.*[109]

At the conclusion of her essay 'All That is You' Irawati describes experiencing a sense of spiritual devastation as she looked back at her life, her career, and all the troubles in Germany, India, and the world:

> *Yes. Yes. My little granddaughter is I. The dog with his wagging tail looking at me with his expressive eyes is I. The cuckoo flying through the limitless blue sky is I. The magnificent evening is I. Eichmann. Stalin. Hitler. Murderers, them who burn down houses, rioters, them who escape from burning houses, them who die in pits. Is I. All of it is I. I am all of it.*
>
> *My confession is done. And at the moment of knowing, I am ashes.*

In non-human existence, there is no morality, and no duality. But morality exists within the human realm, even if it is conditional. And although Irawati was 'reduced to ashes' by her reflection and conclusion about the nature of being, she also knew that, within the confining space and time of human existence, there *are* clear moral and ethical codes dividing the individual person from the 'all': racism, hatred, violence, genocide—we know right from wrong, even when we commit wrongs, even when we allow them to be committed. Here we are separate, and we are, each one of us, responsible for our own actions, and these are, in the narrowest and the broadest senses, identifiable as good or evil. Irawati knew this. It is why she struggled with the meaning and effect of her own actions.

Beyond human existence, the duality of right and wrong, and even of self and not-self have no meaning. All beings belong in a single existence, past, present, future, good and evil: by whomever and however they are defined. We all long to return, and we will return, not to ashes or dust, but to the paramatma—the ultimate, the eternal soul, the One soul, at the beginning, and the end, of all time and all space and all existence. When all the souls have returned to the one, it will be as it was: without time, without space, a simple, single, whole. Alone.

Afterwords

'Truly the universe is full of ghosts, not sheeted churchyard spectres, but the inextinguishable elements of individual life, which having once been, can never die, though they blend and change, and change again for ever.'

—H. Rider Haggard, *King Solomon's Mines*

This biography has two authors—both of whom came to it with very different intentions toward the protagonist, and neither of whom intended to write her biography. Because of this, both of us learned things about Irawati, and also about the research process. These insights and reflections do not belong in the biography of Irawati Karve, but they do belong to this work.

Thiago: So, what moved us to write this book? Umi, why did you want to write a biography about Irawati, your grandmother?

Umi: I actually wanted to write a novel, based in your city—Berlin, about an Indian woman who went there to do her PhD, in the 1920s. It was inspired by Irawati's time there, in that very special period, and I got a grant[110] to do the research for the novel. The timing was such that I was forced to travel during the early days of Covid, when the world was silent, and the museums and libraries were closed. It didn't matter as much to me because writing a novel meant I was interested in the mood of Berlin as much as, or maybe a bit more than, say, the actual building she lived in and the train she took to get to the university (though I did find out those details.) Then Renuka Chatterjee at Speaking Tiger said they were interested in a biography, she thought I was already working on one. At the time I thought I had so much material that I was the logical person to write it. I volunteered. This 'so much material,' I soon realised, was you: early in the course of my research I had contacted Nandini Sundar, who has written a wonderful biography of Iru, and she put me in touch with you. Let's start by saying, without you as a co-author, there would be no biography, nor a novel for that matter. Having undertaken this work I found things that I want people, and my friends and her (my) family to know, about their quite amazing ancestor, as well as, also because of you, about history: what can happen, what can unfold—how one woman going to Germany to study can bring such lasting and deep influence into a whole discipline. It's a frightening, and also exciting example of consequence. My sister (sava saheli singh) asked me, 'Is this a love letter to your grandmother?' to which I replied, 'Why would I write a love letter to someone so long dead? It's to you, to all of you—so you know what I found out, I and Thiago, so you know her, in as much truth as we can convey.' It's been startling, to say the least, what I found out. (Again, I have to thank you for a LOT of this.) We only knew that our grandmother, Irawati Karve, was a well-known anthropologist. Really, that's all we knew! And now I know a lot more about her, and about the world at the time she lived in it, and about the world we live in.

Thiago, why Irawati? Of all the people you could have chosen to research, why her? You, like me, had no idea or intention toward a biography—

Thiago: Irawati stood out as the only researcher at that centre for racial and eugenics research in Berlin (the KWI-A) who came to a conclusion that challenged a racist theory of that time and place, namely, that there the so-called European 'races' would have a more developed right-side of the brain because they were thought to be more intelligent. When I was studying in Germany, I did a research and exhibition about the KWI-A. It was a hard research for me. It was hard to see that so many scientists could so deeply believe, and support, racist and eugenicist ideologies, and to see that they wrote about it with so much scientific conviction. And many of them never realised that their science could have been wrong (as we now know it was—deeply wrong and deeply problematic). So, to see that there was this one person, this young Indian student, who defied her German supervisor's hypothesis and said 'there is no such thing as a racial factor in this skull shape! This variation might possibly come from environmental conditions,' it was fascinating. It made me think a lot about how it sometimes takes that outsider, or someone who is in that minoritized position, to voice out criticism and to challenge a hegemonic way of thinking, and, in this case, to challenge scientific racism, like Irawati did. In some ways, I saw myself in her: I came from Brazil to be trained in social sciences in Germany and I encountered Eurocentric thinking everywhere! So I thought: I want to find out more about this Irawati! And of course, I was intrigued about how she navigated being inserted in this problematic physical anthropological tradition later in her work in India, and how being trained in this kind of knowledge would have left a mark in her research, but also how she tried to make something new out of it and overcome its problems.

Umi: What did you find in India? I know you stayed there a long time, and did many interviews with the family, and with people who had worked with her and had known her. What do you think her legacy is in the field? What do the people in anthropology and sociology in India think her legacy is?

Thiago: Irawati is a big figure in Indian anthropology, especially in Maharashtra. She was part of a small group of anthropologists who contributed immensely to the institutionalisation of this science in the country, in that special historical moment when India became independent and when not just political but also scientific sovereignty was the aim. She did anthropology (and sociology!) in a time when this science strove to achieve a multifaceted and holistic understanding of the human. And she did it very consciously of the urgent political problems around her. So she wrote about many different societal issues, from questions of language and education to the questions of cultural rights of Adivasis to the social situation of women, and she did this in a time when there were not so many trained social scientists in India, so there was a lot to write and research about. And she was also widely read and listened to, so her work had an important political impact. The fact that *Yuganta* is her most famous work (most students of sociology and anthropology in India know it) shows how fruitful it was to apply methods of cultural and gender analysis to study of ancient texts, and how much such ancient texts can be insightful—especially if one takes them in non-dogmatic ways and analyses them for the sake of cultural critique.

My research focused on a more difficult topic, namely, the

impact of German racial anthropology in Irawati's work, and I looked into how she also continued that tradition of physical anthropology and the problems implied in such classification and inherent hierarchisation of social groups through such biologising (and essentialising) ways. This, too, (and she was not alone in this) has left a mark in Indian anthropology. Anthropology, and particularly biological anthropology, is a field of research that still has a lot to discuss if one wants to break away from the troubles of the legacies of racism in science. But the special thing about Irawati is that she also reflected about this, and over the years she adapted her discourse to emphasise the importance of tolerance for, and appreciation of, the multiplicity of ways of being in the world. She praised multiculturalism and the importance of learning from different cultures, religions, traditions. This cultivation of the plurality of human existence is a core contribution of anthropology for society. Irawati embodied this progressive anthropologist spirit especially in the last decades of her life, turning away from an anti-Muslim position taken for a moment in the late 1940s. These ambiguities, the flaws but also the changes in her position are also what made her so human, and such an interesting character. She did not get stuck in a particular time or mindset and she strove to overcome her own limitations in order to better respond to political and ethical challenges. Her work can still be very insightful today if one wants to reflect about how Indian society, or any society, wants to deal in humanising and accommodating ways with gender inequality or cultural and religious diversity. Her non-dogmatic take on Hinduism appears to be especially insightful for the current situation in India. I think her work in *Yuganta*, as well as some of her statements about Hinduism in books like *Kinship Organisation* and *Hindu Society* would have seen her banned in today's India. Her take on whose home India is, for one: 'anyone who calls it home' is not something that some powerful figures in current politics would take kindly to.

How did it feel doing research about your own grandmother, Umi? Did you see yourself in her somehow? Or was there any personal connection to her that made you want to write about?

Umi: Iru died when I was seven years old. What little experience I had with her is now poorly recalled memories of a small child who believed her grandmother disliked her, and found her a nuisance foisted upon her by her youngest, and, I believe, not her most favourite child! Looking for her in archives, in old photographs and also in my adult memory—trying to remember what my mother had said about her for instance—and constructing her from all those bits and pieces—was strange. There is surprisingly little that the family remembers and knows about her. Much I learned from your interviews and conversations with people who knew her or studied her work. And some I learned from reading her own writing. In her Marathi essays, which were not the easiest for me because my Marathi is quite poor—I found clues about her thoughts, where she had been, what she thought and why. I read her words and had glimpses of her existence. I had a few, very rare moments of identifying with her. When she was in Berlin, for example, I think I felt what she might have felt as a brown woman in a white man's territory. But I think she was more confident than I, or at any rate more able to walk tall in the world that she was determined to understand. (She was in fact taller than I am too.) My attraction and revulsion about all things German, particularly the language, was because I heard it so often in my childhood. To me it was what Philippe Sands calls 'the language of concealment and history'—it spoke about the history of my grandparents, and, it was their secret language with each other, secret from everyone else. When I read Iru's essay about migrations of birds and animals and people making her want to wander off because the aeons of ancestral nomads in her blood came alive—I thought about how she left Gauri, my mother, behind so much, and I understood Gauri so much better, and perhaps forgave her a little bit for her frequent abandonment of me and my sisters. My love for our physical world—wild and pet animals, my interest and love for birds and trees and flowers—I received that from my mother, who most certainly received it from Iru. When my partner and I go looking for the resting places of migrating cranes in Germany, I imagine Iru must have done the same, or at least she would have, had she the time and resources. People die, and leave only archives. But I am also an archive of my grandmother's history, I have to trust that. I don't mean it in the way of DNA or blood or anything like that. Just that she was there in my life, herself, but also all around me in the form of my mother who was her daughter, my grandfather who was her partner through her life, my uncles and aunts, cousins, everyone who experienced her, even her books, her house that I lived in. And all through this, I have been conscious that you and I, together, have constructed one picture of someone. It is a precious piece of (history? A woman? Family?), and we have both been vigilant about presenting what we have honestly. I think writing with you has made it possible for me to not write a hagiography, to not erase or embellish. The motivation for this book may not have been what it became through the process—to find that Irawati wherever I can, so we may all know her better, know her at all—but that is the motivation now.

Thiago: Some biographies very easily slip into a heroization (or villainization!) of the main characters they portray, and this was indeed not what we wanted. Irawati had a remarkable life, for sure, and there is a lot to admire in her life and work; but there are also many ambiguities and difficulties in her work, some of them are beyond the realm of her intentions. We wanted to make these ambiguities visible, and present them to the reader, without necessarily overinterpreting them either. Contradictions are everywhere, especially when we look at them from the historical vantage point of the present. Understanding such contradictions from the past helps us move forward, hopefully for the better. Now, apart from finding the right balance in our tone of critique towards this historical actor, one of the challenges we had in writing was the gaps in the archives. There was not much in official archives about Irawati. In fact, there is not much in official archives about most scientists in the Global South, and this is even more true about women in science. The intersection of factors that resulted in such little availability in historical documents about Irawati was a challenge, but there were some documents, and we did navigate this archival scarcity through other methods, which included oral interviews, and reading between-the-lines of her publications and notes. We also walked together in Berlin, seeing and sensing the places where she lived, walked, and worked.

Importantly, we allowed ourselves to fill those gaps with what, echoing Saidiya V. Hartman[111] and others, I would call 'critical fabulation'. Critical fabulation is, to quote the historian of South Asian science Projit Bihari Mukharji, 'a mode of fabulation grounded in rigorous archival research.'[112] It is a way to infer from the available sources and, bridging the gaps, construct narratives on historical actors that would otherwise remain invisible in historiography. For us, this meant that we tried to craft stories from the many pieces and fragmented bits of information we heard or read about Irawati, and about the places and other people she was in contact with. We made a big effort in weaving those stories together, especially when we tried to portray the effective realms in Irawati's life. The everyday stories. The personal feelings and the tensions. All of that made up who she was and, although none of this was in the formal archives, we tried to give an explorative interpretation of it, also based on the stories told by those who knew her. I am, after all, a scientist, an anthropologist, so I constrained myself to writing what was true to this historical person (which I did based on my archival research and on several interviews I conducted with family members, former colleagues, and students of hers), while you did most of the work in putting together family memories and in the reconstructive elaborations. Umi, how was this process for you? As someone who mostly wrote fiction before, what was it like writing about a real person, a historical figure?

Umi: That is exactly right—the physical archives are sparse, as are the memories of living people who knew Irawati, who themselves are now few. I drew on my own life as a Karve, and especially, my mother's memories. As Gauri was a flâneuse of life and a marvellous storyteller, she made her memories mine. You have been especially rigorous in your research, and for me, that has been an invaluable resource on which to base, from which to form, formulate, write, a person and a place that comes as close to Irawati in her time as possible. For us both, being in some of the places she has been—Pune where I was born and lived until she died, Bombay, London, Berlin—helped. For you, of course that's why and that is where it began, in that building in Berlin, and then, your long stays in Pune. The Berlin section is one example of the 'critical fabulation' you talk about: Irawati spent a relatively short time there, but it had a great impact on her life, and on the field. So we agreed that this period warranted a close examination and more representation in the biography even though the time was brief. Even so, we had very little to go on, and we used this form of narrative. This is not new. In 1918, Lytton Strachey published biographies of prominent Victorians including Victoria herself. He changed how biography was written, by constructing a narrative rather than a dry timeline of facts. I would not call it fiction in that it is not an unrestricted, unrestrained free flowing narrative the way writing fiction is for me. It is more like improvisation in music, where both of us were held to the standard that we are playing: we were restricted, or rather, bounded by what was possible, who was possible, and also, importantly, by our own intentions: to present an Irawati Karve constructed from a rigorous, careful, thoughtful, dig. As deep and as wide in the dirt as we could. I won't stretch this analogy too far, but, in a way, this is what we had to do. Reconstruct a person with the tools we had, from the shards and fragments, and yes, the skulls and bones we found. And on that bounded site of Irawati's life, I think there was at least one moment, for both of us, when we asked Irawati, 'Are you me?' or 'Am I you?'

Thanks

From Urmilla Deshpande:

Thiago Pinto Barbosa, brilliant and thoughtful, cheerful, and finally stern, without you this work would not exist.

Renuka Chatterjee, you instigated, nurtured, and perfected this biography.

Chanda Nimbkar, for your trust and belief in me. It was invaluable.

Meithili, for reading every draft with love and microscopic care, even though you had things to build, a garden to weed, and dogs, cats and sometimes children to tend to.

Frank-Udo Tielmann, patient and impatient and present all through this project, all through Germany and India, all through life.

Jan and Chris Maughan, for your loving encouragement. And tea.

Niranjan Rajadhyaksha, thank you old friend, for sharing your knowledge.

Pratibha Kanekar generously shared some of the photographs she had acquired for own her biography of Irawati in Marathi.

Sheila Curran, thank you always for your love, which includes loving what I write, and your care, which includes pineapples.

Michael and Mary Jo Peltier, my Tallahassee family.

Julianna Baggott, who said to have no fear. (And told me to remember that Lytton Strachey wrote Queen Victoria's dying thoughts in his biography of her.)

The research in Berlin was funded by the 'Crossing Borders' program of the Robert Bosch Foundation and the Literarisches Colloquium Berlin (the grant was for the novel that is still in progress).

The Rockefeller Archive Center kindly digitized and provided us Chadbourne Gilpatric and Irawati's papers.

From Thiago Pinto Barbosa:

Co-authoring with Urmilla Deshpande has been a bliss. Thank you, Umi, for reminding me that writing can be joyful and beautiful!

This book is indebted to the many people and institutions that made my research possible, including: my doctoral supervisors and reviewers Katharina Schramm, Banu Subramanian, Heike Liebau; my colleagues at the Anthropology of Global Inequalities Research Group at the University of Bayreuth; my colleagues at Leibniz-Zentrum Moderner Orient in Berlin; the many scholars who commented on earlier drafts of my papers on the topic, in several conferences around the world; MONOM Stiftung für Veränderung; German Historical Institute London; Manuela Bauche and team; all my anthropology teachers, in Brazil and Germany; Yash Gandhi's family for hosting me in Pune; and all the incredibly patient people in India—anthropologists, sociologists, archaeologists, and Karve family members—who shared hours and hours of stories and knowledge with me.

Notes

1 Karve, Irawati. *Kinship Organisation of India*. Poona: Deccan College, 1953.

2 Karve, Irawati. *Hindu Society: An Interpretation*. India: Deshmukh Prakashan, 1968.

3 Karve, Irawati, Yuganta, India: Deshmukh Prakashan, 1967.

4 Karve, Irawati, Gangajal, India: Deshmukh & Co, 1976, p. 121.

5 The following South Asian students were registered at the Berlin University at the same time as Irawati: medicine student Moilanius de Almeida (from Ceylon, today Sri Lanka), geology student Ajit Kumar Banerji (from British India), chemistry student Syed Mahdihassan Hassan (from British India), electric engineering student Kemal Kishan (from British India), and Eknath Mahajani (British India). This list (which is probably not complete) was compiled by Razak Khan based on his research in the archives of the Humboldt University Berlin (Khan, Razak. South Asian Students in Berlin during World War I and the Interwar Period. 2019. Available at: https://www.projekt-mida.de/en/thematicressources/list-of-south-asian-students-in-berlin-during-world-war-i-and-the-interwar-period/.)

6 Jenkins, Jennifer; Liebau, Heike; Schmid, Larissa, Transnationalism and insurrection: independence committees, anti-colonial networks, and Germany's global war. In: Journal of Global History 15 (1), 2020, pp. 61-79.

7 Sands, Philippe. East West Street: on the origins of 'genocide' and 'crimes against humanity'. Vintage, 2017.

8 The word 'Basters' derives from the Dutch word Bastaard, which means crossbreed.

9 Karve, Irawati. *Hindu Society: An Interpretation*. India: Deshmukh Prakashan, 1968, p. 179 n.4.

10 Karve, Irawati, Paripurti, India: Deshmukh & Co, 1949, p. 8.

11 The bust of Nefertiti was found on 6 December 1912 during an excavation at the Middle Egyptian site of Tell el-Amarna. The excavation campaign was led by the Egyptologist and architectural historian Ludwig Borchardt (1863–1938). In the course of the subsequent partage, or division of the finds, the bust was allocated to the German share. The official partage marked the end of the excavation campaign of 1912–1913, which was followed by one last campaign shortly before the outbreak of the First World War. By contract all the finds allotted to the party from Berlin became the property of James Simon, who, in an extraordinarily generous gesture, bequeathed all the finds from Amarna, including the bust of Nefertiti, to the Berlin museum in 1920. (staatliche museen zu berlin, 2024)

12 Translated from the original in German: 'erhielt von Herrn Professor Fischer die Aufgabe, lediglich festzustellen, ob 1. Unterschiede in der rechtsseitigen und linksseitigen Asymmetrie bestehen und 2. Unterschiede in der Häufigkeit der Asymmetrie bei verschiedenen Rassen, speziell bei Europäern und anderen Rassen vorkommen.' Karve, Irawati. Normale Asymmetrie des Menschlichen Schädels: Inaugural-Dissertation. Leipzig: Schwarzenberg & Schumann, 1931, p. 9.

13 Gauri remembers that all of her uncle Ra Dho's published and unpublished books and papers were in the Karve house after he died. He died when Gauri was just twelve years old and, although she was forbidden from reading them, she of course did. One of the characters in her novels asks why, though men bribe, murder, sell children into prostitution, it is women's sexual desires that are called immoral. She attributes this, and her views on women's sexuality to R.D. Karve's writings.

14 Karve, D.D. and Ellen E. McDonald. The New Brahmans: Five Maharashtrian Families. Selected and Translated by DD Karve, with the editorial assistance of Ellen E. McDonald. Berkeley and Los Angeles: University of California Press, 1963, p. 103.

15 Karve, Irawati, Yuganta, India: Deshmukh Prakashan, 1967, p. 92. Free translations by authors.

16 Karve, Irawati, Yuganta, India: Deshmukh Prakashan, 1967, p. 93. Free translations by authors.

17 Deshpande, Gauri. The Lackadaisical Sweeper: Short Stories. India: Manas, 1997, pp. 141-162.

18 Karve, D.D. and Ellen E. McDonald. *The New Brahmans: Five Maharashtrian Families.* Selected and Translated by D.D. Karve, with the editorial assistance of Ellen E. McDonald. Berkeley and Los Angeles: University of California Press, 1963.

19 Karve, D.D. and Ellen E. McDonald. *The New Brahmans: Five Maharashtrian Families.* Selected and Translated by D.D. Karve, with the editorial assistance of Ellen E. McDonald. Berkeley and Los Angeles: University of California Press, 1963.

20 Interview with Gouri Salvi, 1989, as published in; Deshpande, Gauri, *Deliverance*, translated by Shashi Deshpande, Women Unlimited, New Delhi, 2010, p.129.

21 Karve, Irawati, Paripurti, India: Deshmukh & Co, 1949, pp. 25-29.

22 Karve, Irawati, Paripurti, India: Deshmukh & Co, 1949, pp. 7-12.

23 Karve, Irawati, Paripurti, India: Deshmukh & Co, 1949, pp. 137-139.

24 Karve, Irawati. 'The Indian Women in 1975.' *Perspective, supplement to the Indian Journal of public administration* 1, 1966, pp. 103-135.

25 Karve, Irawati. Kinship Organisation in India. Poona: Deccan College, 1953.

26 Karve, Irawati. Kinship Organisation in India. Poona: Deccan College, 1953, p. 179.

27 Karve, Irawati. 'The Indian Women in 1975.' *Perspective,*

supplement to the Indian Journal of public administration 1, 1966, p 107.

28 Karve, Irawati. 'The Indian Women in 1975.' *Perspective, supplement to the Indian Journal of public administration* 1, 1966, p 121.

29 Karve, Irawati. 'The Indian Women in 1975.' *Perspective, supplement to the Indian Journal of public administration* 1, 1966, p.21.

30 Karve, Irawati, Sanskruti, India: Deshmukh & Co, 1972, pp. 114-171.

31 Karve, Irawati, Sanskruti, India: Deshmukh & Co, 1972.

32 The god Vitthal, a form of Vishnu or Krishna, and very important in the cultural history of Maharashtra (Maharashtra—land and its People, Karve, Dr. (Mrs.) I., Maharashtra State Gazetteer, 1968., p.188)

33 Lokmanya Bal Gangadhar Tilak, Gopal Ganesh Agarkar, Mahadev Govind Ranade.

34 A recollection from the archives of the Royal Anthropological Institute: 'Mrs Karvé was involved in the collection of anthropometrical data in India, and desperately needed a calculating machine. Dr Jack C. Trevor arranged for a second-hand Monroe to be sent to her from Cambridge University, but it seems to have spent most of its time in an Indian Customs House. It was dispatched in August 1946, and at the end of March 1947 we hear that it has been in customs for two months, and still they are waiting for some paper-work to be settled. Once her studentship had finished, and the machine was to be sent back, it was again held up over an export-permit.' (Sarah Walpole—Archivist and Photo Curator, Royal Anthropological Institute, From the Archives: Trials and Tribulations of Horniman Scholars, © 2024 Royal Anthropological Institute).

35 See: Mukharji, Projit Bihari. *Brown skins, white coats: Race science in India, 1920-66.* Chicago: The University of Chicago Press, 2023.

36 Guha, A. (2021). Nation Building on the Margins: How the Anthropologists of India Contributed? Sociological Bulletin, 70(1), 59-75. https://doi.org/10.1177/0038022920956753

37 Charles Cornwallis, 1st Marquess and 2nd Earl Cornwallis (born December 31, 1738, London, England—died October 5, 1805, Ghazipur, India [now in Uttar Pradesh, India]) was a British soldier and statesman, probably best known for his defeat at Yorktown, Virginia, in the last important campaign (September 28–October 19, 1781) of the American Revolution. Cornwallis was possibly the most capable British general in that war, but he was more important for his achievements as British governor-general of India (1786–93, 1805) and viceroy of Ireland (1798–1801). (Britannica, T. Editors of Encyclopaedia. 'Charles Cornwallis, 1st Marquess and 2nd Earl Cornwallis.' Encyclopedia Britannica, May 17, 2024. https://www.britannica.com/biography/Charles-Cornwallis-1st-Marquess-and-2nd-Earl-Cornwallis.)

38 The theory that different jatis originated from the splitting of different varnas was one that many scholars in Karve's time defended, including her first mentor Ghurye.

39 For a critical analysis of Karve's physical anthropology of Maharashtrians, see: Barbosa, Thiago P. Racializing a New Nation: German Coloniality and Anthropology in Maharashtra, India. In *Perspectives on Science* 30 (1), 2022, pp. 137-166.

40 Karve, Irawati. Kinship Organisation in India. Poona: Deccan College, 1953, p. 19

41 Karve, Irawati. Kinship Organisation in India. Poona: Deccan College, 1953, p. 19.

42 Malhotra credits Irawati with many intrusions into his career, ones that changed the course of his work, and also his life. He recalls how he, as a shy twenty-year-old, met Irawati Karve, for the first time. It was 1961, when she was a large personality in the field. He was a student at the department of anthropology in New Delhi University, where he was doing his PhD, and also ran a tutoring school. One day, much to his chagrin,

he heard that the department head P.C. Biswas was looking for him. This was usually not a good thing, and Malhotra hurried to the office to be told that Irawati Karve needed a research assistant for field work in South India, and it was an opportunity not to be missed. He was not given much of a choice, and, in three days Malhotra packed up his things, said goodbye to his family, and left for Pune. The research trip went smoothly, and Malhotra very much enjoyed the time with colleagues on the road and being in places he had never been before. Two months later, back in Pune, he had a few days before he headed home, when another professor from Delhi University contacted him and asked if he would gather data on Chitpavans since he was there in Maharashtra. He agreed, and began to wander the streets by bicycle looking for light-eyed people, who he knew were likely to be Chitpavans. 'Have you been in Pune before?' Irawati asked him when she heard of this enterprise, and Malhotra laughed and said, 'I had never left the Indo-Gangetic plain before.' She was amazed as well as amused that this young man was spending his time there collecting data rather than relaxing and sightseeing. She arranged for him to meet the principal of Wadia College in Pune, who in turn set him up with a desk and a chair and instructed all Chitpavan students to report to him. His job was done in two days, and, or so he thought, he would now have the time to relax and sightsee. Then he got word that Irawati Bai was looking for him. Again with some trepidation he went to Deccan College, and found that, again, he was being asked to go on a trip—this time 40 kilometres away from Pune, to Chandoli, where Sankalia himself had found a human skeleton. He was excited. These two people were already legends in the field, and it was an immense opportunity for him. But, he was not clear or sure that this was what he wanted. He was too shy to refuse, though he tried to tell them that he did not have the experience to handle human remains, that he would make mistakes, that he had a life to get back to in New Delhi. The two professors, who were clearly very close, and in this case seemed to be in cahoots, said he had enough time to go back and take care of his affairs. He saw that he would have to comply. 'Who will pay for your ticket?' Irawati asked him, and he replied that he would of course. 'No,' she said, 'I will, and I will give you a job to do while you are there.' Malhotra was to bring back data for her on 'marriage distance.' Meaning, how far do people go to find marriage partners. He discovered that this seemingly small bit of data contained a wealth of information within it, and that half-day's work would change the course of his own research in the later years of his career. When he had finished his report on the human remains at Chandoli, Irawati convinced him to do his PhD with her. Irawati had a sociological hypothesis that she wanted tested with biological materials. The Hindu caste system—varna- is a sociological category, and not a biological one. The studies done by Malhotra, as well as R.K. Gulati (who tested the theory on another endogamous caste, the Kumbhars) support that caste is not a biological, but a sociological category. The summary is included in a new chapter in the second edition of Irawati's *Hindu Society*. Irawati grew to depend on Malhotra. They wrote and published papers together, and, because Irawati was not the best organised person, Malhotra often helped her with administrative tasks. He also took dictation—with a dictionary to check his spellings because his English was not perfect. He looked upon his time with her as productive and formative, and he developed a great fondness for her. Irawati was just as fond of him, this shy and brilliant young man. 'Malhotra' was a name often heard in Irawati's home. Irawati talked about him, and also narrated various incidents about him, including the scandal that had ensued when Malhotra was forced to go on a field trip alone with a woman student, because the other students never showed up. This lady became Mrs. Malhotra. Kailash Chandra Malhotra could have had no inkling of how drastically his life would change when, on one January day in 1960, he was dispatched as a temporary research assistant to Irawati. His work on the Nandiwalas, the group that he continued to study for many years, and on whom he wrote many insightful papers, began with the morsel of meat that Irawati accepted from their headman. Six years later, Malhotra took part in sacrificing two pigs with the Nandiwalas.

43 K.C. Malhotra and R.K.Gulati worked on the Dhangar project.

44 Meaning 'children of God'—a term first used by Gandhi to refer to Dalits in 1932.

45 Karve, Irawati. Paripurti, India: Deshmukh & Co, 1949, pp. 71-78.

46 Karve, Irawati. *Bhovara.* Poona: Deshmukh & Co, 1960.

47 Sankalia, H.D. *Born for Archaeology: An Autobiography.* India: B.R., 1970, p. 33.

48 MacCurdy, George Grant. *Human origins: A manual of prehistory.* Vol. 2. D. Appleton, 1924.

49 Sankalia, H.D. Born for Archaeology: An Autobiography. India: B.R., 1970, p. 51.

50 Sankalia, H.D. Born for Archaeology: An Autobiography. India: B.R., 1970, p.112.

51 Karve, Irawati. *Paripurti*, Poona: Deshmukh & Co, 1949, p. 19.

52 Karve, Irawati. *Paripurti*, Poona: Deshmukh & Co, 1949, pp. 20-24.

53 Karve, Irawati. *Bhovara.* Poona: Deshmukh & Co, 1960, pp. 128-135.

54 Karve, Irawati, *Gangajal*, Poona: Deshmukh & Co, 1976, pp 71-75.

55 Karve, Irawati. Kinship Organisation in India. Poona: Deccan College, 1953.

56 Christoph Haimendorf's work is quoted or mention in several pages of Irawati's book *Kinship Organisation* (Karve, Irawati. *Kinship Organisation of India.* Poona: Deccan College, 1953, pp. 183, 240, 248, 277, 278).

57 Karve, Irawati. *Kinship Organisation of India.* Poona: Deccan College, 1953, p. xi.

58 Karve, Irawati. *Kinship Organisation of India*. Poona: Deccan College, 1953, p. xi.

59 See: Salvucci, Daniela, Elisabeth Tauber & Dorothy L. Zinn. 'The Malinowskis in South Tyrol: A Relational Biography of People, Places and Works' *Bérose—Encyclopédie internationale des histoires de l'anthropologie*, Paris, 2019.

60 Karve, Irawati. *Kinship Organization in India*. 2nd ed. Bombay: Asia Pub., 1965, p. 388.

61 Clyde Kluckhohn (1905–1960) was Professor of Anthropology at Harvard University and Curator of Southwestern American Ethnology at Harvard's Peabody Museum.

62 Diary of Chadbourne Gilpatric, Rockefeller Foundation records, Projects, SG 1.2, Series 300-833, Latin America, Europe, Africa, Asia, Oceania (FA387b); India, Series 464 ; India—Humanities and Arts , Subseries 464.RBox/Reel: Box 7 4; Folder/Frame: Folder 728; Folder Title: Deccan College—Karve, lrawati, 1952-1953; Date: 1952-1953

63 Ibid.

64 A partial list of scholars Irawati planned to meet: F.S.C. Northrop, Department of Philosophy, Yale University, New Haven, Connecticut; Robert Crane, Department of History, University of Chicago, Illinois; Melville Herskovitz, Department of Anthropology, Northwestern University, Evanston, Illinois; Ruth Hill Useem and John Useem, Michigan State University, Lansing, Michigan; Maureen L.P. Patterson, South Asian Program, University of Pennsylvania (who had read every published word of Irawati's and worked closely with her); William Norman Brown, University of Pennsylvania; Horace Pohlman, Library of Congress, Washington DC; Cora Dubois and Clare Holt, Institute of International Education, Washington DC; Morris Opler, Department of Sociology and Anthropology, Cornell University, Ithaca NY; Murray Emmenau, Department of Linguistics, UC Berkely; David Mandelbaum, Department of Anthropology, UC Berkeley; A.L. Kroeber, Department of Anthropology, UC Berkeley;

Abraham Kaplan, Department of Philosophy, UCLA; Harry Hoijer, Department of Anthropology, UCLA.

65 Morris E. Opler, Cornell University, Ithaca.

66 Karve, Irawati, Yuganta, India: Deshmukh Prakashan, 1967, p. 165. Free translations by authors.

67 The narrators of the Puranas were also sutas. The Mahabharata, the Ramayana and the Puranas have been called sauta literature by Dr. S. V. Ketkar, that is, literature belonging to the sutas, preserved, sung, and largely composed by them. (Karve, Irawati, Yuganta, India: Deshmukh Prakashan, 1967, pp. 4-5.)

68 For a detailed analysis of this controversy, see: Barbosa, Thiago P.: Indian Sociology and Anthropology Between a Decolonizing Quest and the West: Thinking with the case of Irawati Karve. *Revue d'histoire des sciences humaines* (41): 181-211.

69 Hutton, J.H. 'Review of 'Kinship Organisation in India', by Irawati Karvé.' *Man* 54, 1954, pp. 159-60; Useem, John. 'Review of 'Kinship Organisation in India', by Irawati Karve.' *American Anthropologist* 59 (4), 1957, pp. 737-39.

70 Sundar, Nandini. In the Cause of Anthropology: The Life and Work of Irawati Karve. In Patricia Uberoi, Nandini Sundar, Satish Deshpande (Eds.): Anthropology in the East: Founders of Indian sociology and anthropology. Calcutta: Seagull, 2008, p. 396, emphasis added.

71 Dumont, Louis, and D.F. Pocock. 'Review of I. Karve's Kinship Organisation in India.' *Contributions to Indian Sociology* 1, no. 1 (1957): 43-64.

72 Dumont, Louis. *Homo Hierarchicus: Le Système des Castes et ses Implications.* Paris: Gallimard, 1966.

73 See: Madan, T.N. 'For a Sociology of India.' *Contributions to Indian Sociology*, no. 9, 1966, pp. 9-16; Das, Veena. *Critical Events: An Anthropological Perspective on Contemporary India.* Oxford India paperbacks. Delhi: Oxford University Press, 2018.

74 See, for example: Willkerson, Isabel. Caste: The Origins of Our Discontents. New York: Random House, 2020.

75 For a detailed analysis of the Dumont versus Karve controversy, see: Barbosa, Thiago P. Indian Sociology and Anthropology Between a Decolonising Quest and the West. Thinking with the Case of Irawati Karve. In Revue d'histoire des sciences humaines (41), 2022, pp. 181–211.

76 Karve, Irawati. *Kinship Organization in India.* 2nd ed. Bombay: Asia Pub., 1965, p. 23, emphasis added.

77 Karve, Irawati Karmarkar. Hindu Society: An Interpretation. India: Deshmukh Prakashan, 1968.

78 See: Wulff, Helena. Writing anthropology. In: Stein, Felix (Ed.). *The Open Encyclopedia of Anthropology.* Facsimile of the first edition in *The Cambridge Encyclopedia of Anthropology*, (2021) 2023. Available at: http://doi.org/10.29164/21writing.

79 Karve, Irawati. *Kinship Organization in India.* 2nd ed. Bombay: Asia Pub., 1965, p. 24, emphasis added

80 Karve, Irawati. *Kinship Organization in India.* India: Asia Publishing House, 1954, p. v.

81 Many of the recollections of Berkely are taken from Irawati's own words in her essay, free translation by authors: Karve, Irawati. *Paripurti*, Poona: Deshmukh & Co, 1949, 'Prawas Sampla' (Journey's End)

82 Letter from Melville Herskovits to Chadbourne Gilpatric, Rockefeller Foundation records, Projects, SG 1.2, Series 300-833, Latin America, Europe, Africa, Asia, Oceania (FA387b); India, Series 464 ; India—Humanities and Arts , Subseries 464. RBox/Reel: Box 7 4; Folder/Frame: Folder 728; Folder Title: Deccan College—Karve, lrawati, 1952-1953; Date: 1952-1953

83 Letter from Irawati Karve to Chadbourne Gilpatric, Rockefeller Foundation records, Projects, SG 1.2, Series 300-833, Latin America, Europe, Africa, Asia, Oceania (FA387b); India, Series 464 ; India—Humanities and Arts , Subseries 464.RBox/Reel: Box 7 4; Folder/Frame: Folder 728; Folder Title: Deccan College—Karve, lrawati, 1952-1953; Date: 1952-1953

84 Karve, Irawati. *Hindu Society: An Interpretation*. India: Deshmukh Prakashan, 1968.

85 Deshpande, Gauri. 'Rose Jam,' The Lackadaisical Sweeper: Short Stories. India: Manas, 1997, p. 160.

86 Karve, Irawati, Gangajal, Poona: Deshmukh & Co, 1976, p. 113.

87 Karve, Irawati. *Bhovara*. Poona: Deshmukh & Co, 1960, translation by Urmilla Deshpande, pp. 30-31.

88 Karve, Irawati. Racial conflict. In D.N. Majumdar, Irawati Karve (Eds.): *Racial Problems in Asia*. New Delhi: Indian Council of World Affairs, 1947, pp. 27-54. For a critical analysis of Karve's anti-Muslim accents in that text, see: Barbosa, Thiago P. Racializing a New Nation: German Coloniality and Anthropology in Maharashtra, India. In *Perspectives on Science* 30 (1), 2022, pp. 137-166.

89 Karve, Irawati. 1963. 'The Racial Factor in Indian Social Life.' History Summer School on Indian social history, p. 10

90 M.S. Golwalkar was the head of the Hindu supremacist paramilitary organisation Rashtriya Swayamsevak Sangh (RSS) who was very much inspired by Hitler and whose philosophy was 'Hinduism not Socialism.' See: Basu, Anustup. *Hindutva as political monotheism*. Durham: Duke University Press, 2020.

91 Karve, Irawati, Paripurti, India: Deshmukh & Co, 1949, p. 52.

92 Karve, Irawati. 1963. 'The Racial Factor in Indian Social Life.' History Summer School on Indian social history, p. 9.

93 Karve, Irawati, Paripurti, India: Deshmukh & Co, 1949, pp 51-52.

94 Karve, Irawati. *Bhovara*. Poona: Deshmukh & Co, 1960, p. 49.

95 Karve, Irawati. *Bhovara*. Poona: Deshmukh & Co, 1960, p.25.

96 Karve, Irawati. *Amchi Sanskruti*. Poona: Deshmukh, 1960.

97 One of the many names Vithoba is called by, including, among others, Vithai (where he is the mother Vitthal), and Pandurang.

98 In the English editions of *Yuganta*, Irawati credits Maxine Berntsen as one of the translators, calling Maxine her

'American daughter'. Both had met in the US when Irawati was a guest professor in Philadelphia, and Maxine was the only student in her Marathi course. Maxine was in India for socio-linguistic research and went to Phaltan in 1966 at Irawati's suggestion that she study Marathi variations there. She continued to live there, establishing two schools, writing Marathi textbooks with Jai, and finally, in 1978, became an Indian citizen. Maxine lives today in Hyderabad. She also co-edited, with the South Asia expert and Irawati's lifelong friend Eleanor Zelliot (1926-2016), the collection of essays with the title *The Experience of* Hinduism (Zelliot, Eleanor and Maxine Berntsen. *The Experience of Hinduism: essays on religion in Maharashtra.* Albany, N.Y.: State University of New York Press, 1988). In it, they wrote: 'This volume is a tribute to Irawati Karve…an acknowledgement that all of us—anthropologist, sociologist, political scientist, historian of religion, writer and student alike—are in her debt' (p. xv). The volume builds, she says, 'on the insights of Karve's essays rather than the academic findings of her scholarly work' (p. xvi). Although Irawati's research and academic work was not directly about religion, Zelliot says that the 'multi-colored image of contemporary religion in the Marathi-speaking area' is shaped 'largely due to Irawati Karve's curiosity and energy, to her honesty, to her ability to probe new ways of thinking, to her impatience with the trite or the obvious' (p. xvi).

99 Karve, Irawati. On the Road: A Maharashtrian Pilgrimage (translated from the Marathi by Jai Nimbkar). In: Zelliot, Eleanor and Maxine Berntsen. *The Experience of Hinduism: essays on religion in Maharashtra.* Albany, N.Y.: State University of New York Press, 1988, p. 169.

100 Karve, Irawati. On the Road: A Maharashtrian Pilgrimage (translated from the Marathi by Jai Nimbkar). In: Zelliot, Eleanor and Maxine Berntsen. *The Experience of Hinduism: essays on religion in Maharashtra.* Albany, N.Y.: State University of New York Press, 1988, p. 170.

101 Karve, Irawati. A Town Without a Temple. (translated from the Marathi by Jai Nimbkar). In: Zelliot, Eleanor and Maxine Berntsen. *The Experience of Hinduism: essays on religion in Maharashtra.* Albany, N.Y.: State University of New York Press, 1988, pp. 69-75.

102 Karve, Irawati. A Town Without a Temple. (translated from the Marathi by Jai Nimbkar). In: Zelliot, Eleanor and Maxine Berntsen. *The Experience of Hinduism: essays on religion in Maharashtra.* Albany, N.Y.: State University of New York Press, 1988, p. 72.

103 'Eichmann pleads innocence'—The Statesman, April 12, 1961 'Eichmann defends self in court'—The Hindu, April 13, 1961.

104 Karve, Irawati. 'All that is you': An essay. (translated from the Marathi by Jai Nimbkar). In: Zelliot, Eleanor and Maxine Berntsen. *The Experience of Hinduism: essays on religion in Maharashtra.* Albany, N.Y.: State University of New York Press, 1988, p. 216.

105 Karve, Irawati. 'All that is you': An essay. (translated from the Marathi by Jai Nimbkar). In: Zelliot, Eleanor and Maxine Berntsen. *The Experience of Hinduism: essays on religion in Maharashtra.* Albany, N.Y.: State University of New York Press, 1988, p. 221.

106 Karve, Irawati. [Gratulationsbrief zum 80. Geburtstag von Eugen Fischer]. Verschuer Nachlass, III. Abteilung, Rep. 86A, Number 52, Archive of the Max Planck Society, Berlin-Dahlem.

107 Among other sources, Irawati writes about time in her essay 'Dikkal' (Troubles) Gauri's words are from this essay. Free translation by authors: Karve, Irawati. *Paripurti*, Poona: Deshmukh & Co, 1949.

108 Constantin P. Cavafy, 'The God Abandons Antony' 1911.

109 Karve, Irawati Karmarkar. *Hindu Society: An Interpretation.* India: Deshmukh Prakashan, 1968, pp. 86-88.

110 The research in Berlin was funded by the 'Crossing Borders'

program of the Robert Bosch Foundation and the Literarisches Colloquium Berlin.

111 Hartman, Saidiya. 'Venus in Two Acts.' *Small Axe* 12:2, 2008, pp. 1-14.

112 Mukharji, Projit Bihari. *Brown skins, white coats: Race science in India, 1920-66*. Chicago: The University of Chicago Press, 2023, p. 24.

Daughter of two families: Irawati's father, Ganesh Hari Karmakar (top left), R.P. Paranjpye and Saitai (top right), and above, Irawati with Shakuntala Paranjpye

All Photos Courtesy Urmilla Deshpande

Irawati, aged 16, September 1921 (left) and (below) Irawati and Dinu Karve, Pune 1928—possibly a wedding photograph

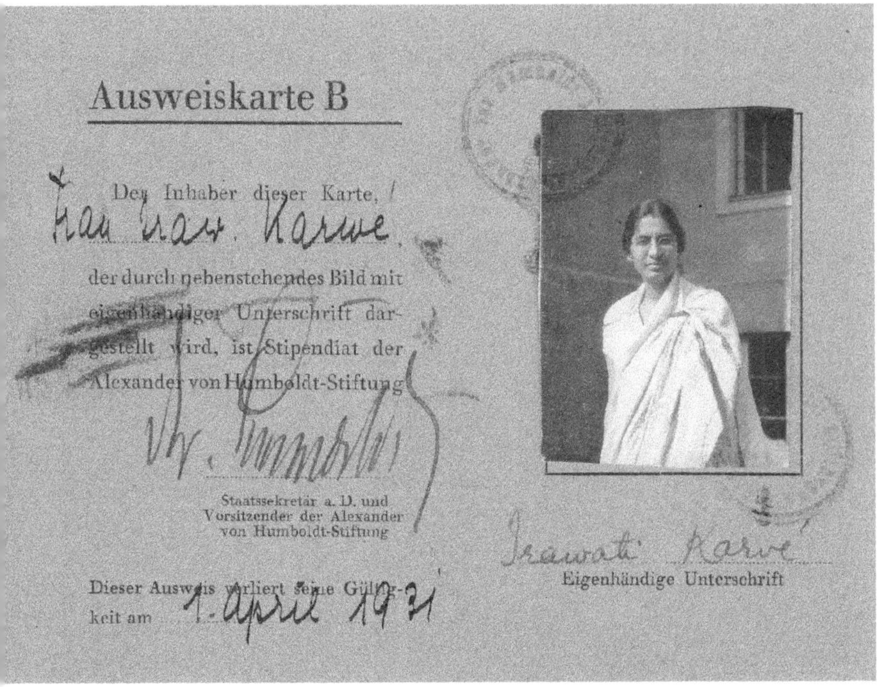

Ausweiskarte B

Der Inhaber dieser Karte, Frau Irav. Karve, der durch nebenstehendes Bild mit eigenhändiger Unterschrift dargestellt wird, ist Stipendiat der Alexander von Humboldt-Stiftung

Staatssekretär a. D. und Vorsitzender der Alexander von Humboldt-Stiftung

Irawati Karve
Eigenhändige Unterschrift

Dieser Ausweis verliert seine Gültigkeit am 1. April 1931

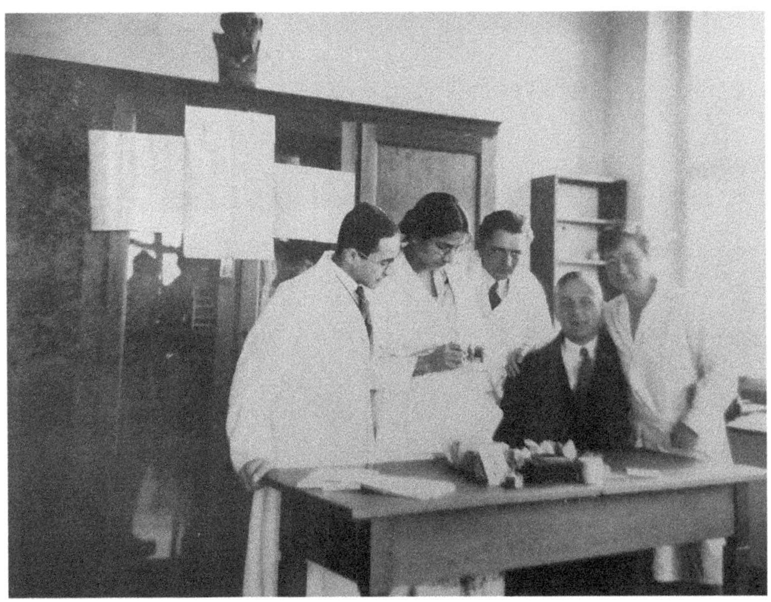

Irawati's ID card from the Humboldt Foundation, valid until April 1931 (top of page) and (above) Irawati with colleagues at KWI-A, Berlin, 1929

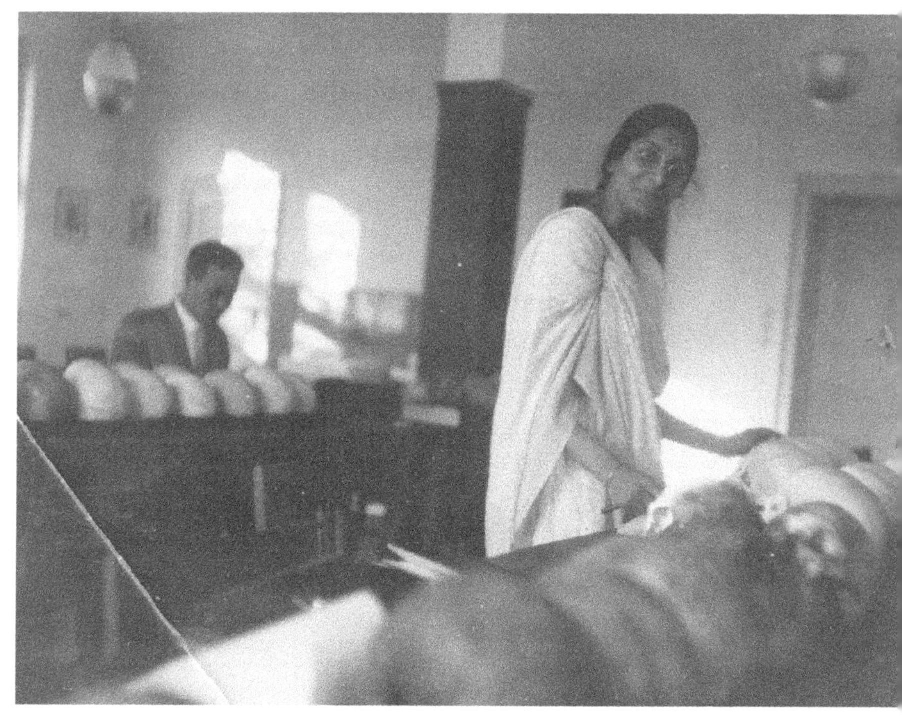

Skulls and bones: Irawati at the KWI-A receiving room with human skulls, Berlin, 1928

Irawati, with her father-in-law Maharshi Karve and Prof. Eugen Fischer, possibly taken when Maharshi Karve was passing through Berlin on his tour of educational institutions in 1929-1930 (left) and (below) Eugen Fischer (front row) with his family, Berlin, sent to Irawati in the 1930s

Putting down roots: Irawati and Dinu at the house at Law College Road, Pune, 1931

Jai and Anand Karve, Pune, 1941 (left) and Gauri Karve, (right) Pune, 1954

Off to work: Irawati with her Lambretta scooter, Pune, 1950 (top of page) and the newly built house in Gultekdi, Pune, 1966, (above)

Family matters: front row (left to right) Nandini Nimbkar, Jai, Dinu, Irawati, Gauri, Manju. Back row (left to right) Bon, Nandu, Gudrun, Avinash Deshpande (Gauri's husband at the time), Pune, 1962

Front row (left to right) Dinu, Maharshi Karve, Bhagirathi Karmarkar (Irawati's mother), Irawati. Back row (left to right) Bon Nimbkar holding Manju Nimbkar, Jai Nimbkar, Gauri holding Nandini Nimbkar, Pune, 1958

Anthropologist at work: Irawati with human remains from the Mesolthic period, Langhnaj, Gujarat, February 1944

With help from the family: Irawati and her brother testing blood samples while her mother, father and sister-in-law look on, Hyderabad, date unknown

On site: Irawati and H.D. Sankalia (front left) with students and colleagues, possibly at a dig site in Gujarat, 1943 (above)

Dual role: Irawati cooking on site, date and place unknown (above)

At home and abroad: Irawati and Christoph Haimendorf, SOAS, London, 1952, (above), and (below) Irawati (middle) with Gauri (l) and Maxine Berntsen (r) at the Gultekdi house, Pune, December 1966

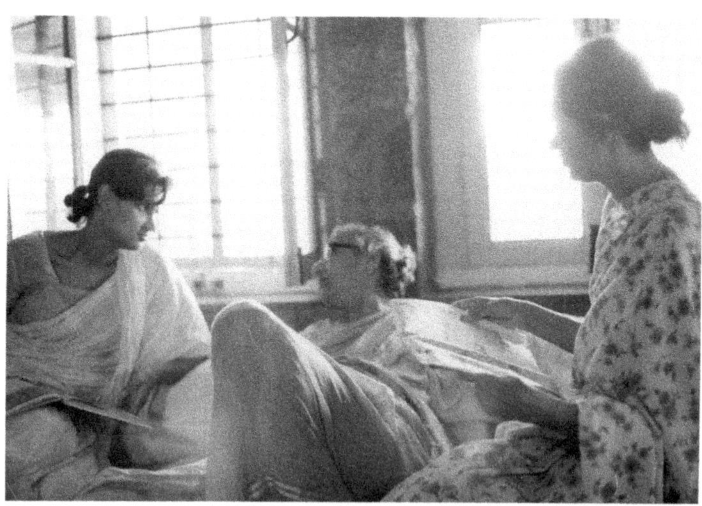

On foreign shores: Irawati, Grand Canyon, Arizona, 1952, (right), and (below) at Berkeley, California, 1960.

Irawati with Kailash Chandra Malhotra (left) and Dr. R.L. Kirk (Human Geneticist from Australia) (above) and (below) with President Zakir Hussain at the Sahitya Akademi Award reception, New Delhi, 1968

Moments of solitude: Irawati on the terrace of her Gultekdi house, Pune, 1966, (above) and (below) walking on the beach

Lifelong companions: Irawati and Dinu in their garden in Pune, 1970

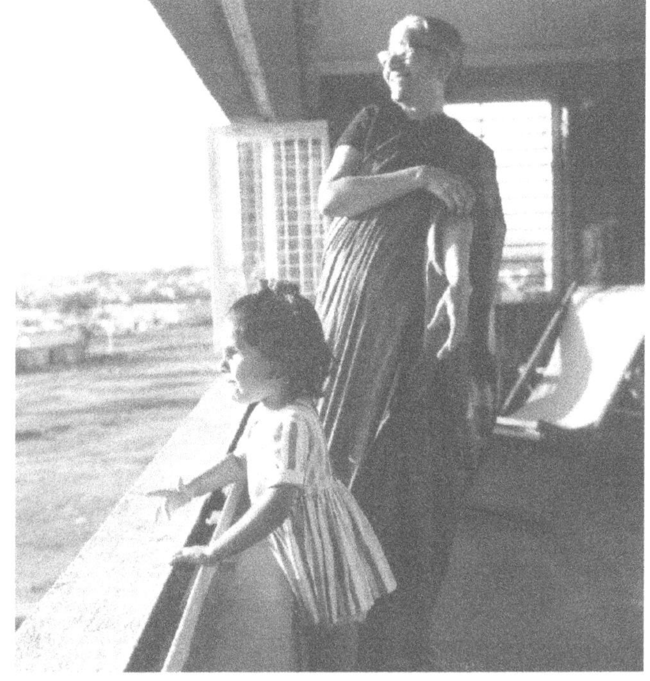

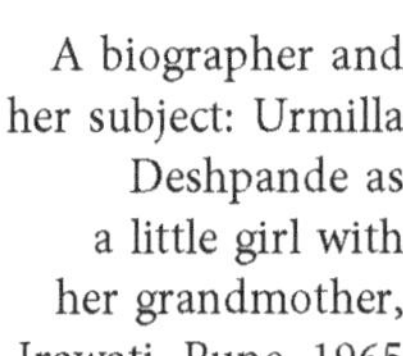

A biographer and her subject: Urmilla Deshpande as a little girl with her grandmother, Irawati, Pune, 1965

Milton Keynes UK
Ingram Content Group UK Ltd.
UKHW040023101224
452185UK00004B/290

9 789354 478475